"This is the kind of book that needs to be read, re-read, and read again—preferably outdoors, where we will find the deepest mysteries of creaturehood in company with Pope Francis and St. Thomas Aquinas. Each creature is a poignantly treasured theophany for Thompson. In wonderfully accessible prose, he leads us from common sense to Catholic truth and back again, showing that the paths of theology and philosophy run through forests, fields, and farms. This book is an awakening."

— MATTHEW LEVERING —
James N. and Mary D. Perry Jr. Chair of
Theology, Mundelein Seminary

"With remarkable clarity and poetic flare, Christopher Thompson gives us the philosophical and theological roots of an environmental ethic so desperately needed today. Deeply grounded in an order of creation informed by natural law and revelation, he weaves a challenging argument that all creation is the embodiment of God's wisdom that reveals not only the goodness of the environment but a common home where all things are connected. One of the powerful underlying implication of this interconnection for Thompson is an integral ecology that helps us to overcome the partial and fragmented accounts of Catholic moral teaching and points to the organic relationships among life, marriage and sexuality, economics, and the environment. In recovering creation, we discover the moral fabric that binds us to each creature, to each other, and to God."

—MICHAEL NAUGHTON —
Director of the Center for Catholic Studies and Koch Chair in Catholic Studies, University of St. Thomas (Minnesota)

"*The Joyful Mystery* engages environmental concerns guided by the wisdom of St. Thomas and in light of God's presence as a loving Creator. A nicely integrated perspective that makes a vital contribution to the contemporary discussion."

— DAVID L. SCHINDLER —
Gagnon Professor of Fundamental Theology, The John Paul II Institute, Washington DC

"If, like me, you are one of those readers who underlines books and scribbles notes in the margin, then you'd best get two copies of Christopher Thompson's *The Joyful Mystery*, one to mark up and one that you'll still be able to read later on. It is an immensely rich, well-researched book that makes beautifully clear that Catholics should be leading the environmental movement, rather than trailing behind."

— BENJAMIN WIKER —
Professor of Political Science and Director of Human Life Studies, Franciscan University of Steubenville and author of *In Defense of Nature*

·᛫᛭᛫·

LIVING FAITH

SERIES EDITOR: FR. DAVID VINCENT MECONI, S.J.
Fr. David Vincent Meconi, S.J., is a Jesuit priest and professor of theology at Saint Louis University where he also serves as the Director of the Catholic Studies Centre. He is the editor of *Homiletic and Pastoral Review* and has published widely in the areas of Church history and Catholic culture. He holds the pontifical license in Patristics from the University of Innsbruck in Austria, and the D.Phil. in Ecclesiastical History from the University of Oxford.

ABOUT THE SERIES

The great Christian Tradition has always affirmed that the world in which we live is a reflection of its divine source, a place perhaps torn apart by sin but still charged with busy and bustling creatures disclosing the beautiful presence of God. The *Living Faith* series consists of eminent Catholic authors who seek to help Christians navigate their way in this world. How do we understand objective truth in a culture insistent on relativism? How does one evangelize in a world offended when invited to something higher? How do we understand sin and salvation when so many have no real interest in becoming saints? The *Living Faith* series will answer these and numerous other questions Christians have today as they set out not only to live holy lives themselves, but to bring others to the fullness of life in Christ Jesus.

THE JOYFUL MYSTERY

THE JOYFUL MYSTERY

Field Notes Toward a Green Thomism

CHRISTOPHER J. THOMPSON

EMMAUS
ROAD
PUBLISHING

Steubenville, Ohio
www.emmausroad.org

Emmaus Road Publishing
1468 Parkview Circle
Steubenville, Ohio 43952

©2017 Christopher J. Thompson
All rights reserved. Second Printing 2022
Printed in the United States of America

Library of Congress Cataloging-in-Publication Data
Names: Thompson, Christopher J. (Christopher James), author.
Title: The joyful mystery : field notes toward a green Thomism / Christopher J. Thompson.
Description: Steubenville : Emmaus Road Pub., 2017. | Series: Living faith
Identifiers: LCCN 2017031032 (print) | LCCN 2017031536 (ebook) | ISBN 9781945125638 (ebook) | ISBN 9781945125614 (hardcover) | ISBN 9781945125621 (pbk.)
Subjects: LCSH: Human ecology--Religious aspects--Catholic Church. | Ecotheology. | Catholic Church. Pope (2013- : Francis). Laudato si'. | Thomas, Aquinas, Saint, 1225?-1274. | Catholic Church--Doctrines.
Classification: LCC BX1795.H82 (ebook) | LCC BX1795.H82 T46 2017 (print) | DDC 241/.691--dc23
LC record available at https://lccn.loc.gov/2017031032

Cover image: ©Andrew_Howe / istockphoto.com
Cover design and layout by Margaret Ryland

and Thou shalt not despise
Even me, the priest of this poor sacrifice.

To Nature, Samuel Taylor Coleridge

TABLE OF CONTENTS

PREFACE

THE privilege of teaching for nearly three decades in Catholic venues has led me to believe that one of the greatest challenges—perhaps the greatest challenge—to an effective evangelization lies in overcoming the loss of confidence in the splendor of creation and its capacity to disclose something fundamentally meaningful; that is, to disclose the reality of God. My efforts in this book should be taken as a plea and a prayer for a much deeper agenda than merely promoting a consideration of the environment: to recover the joyful mystery of the cosmos and thus set in motion the only conditions in which a renewed, authentic Catholic culture can emerge.

For here, and only here, squarely within this temple of creation, a Catholic culture takes root; the good news of Jesus Christ moves from its conceptual power to its cultural expression; heaven and earth are wed in the physical body of the believer, the mystical body of believers; and the plan of the Incarnation takes root in a geography— before it ever takes shape in history.

Christianity is the lived claim that each one of us, as embodied creatures occupying a glorious cosmos, has been invited to a friendship with the Maker of it all. A bold exchange of an eternal friendship between the embodied human person and the divinity itself has been made available in the person of Jesus Christ. Christ, the Christians proclaim, is the Logos made flesh, the very same Logos who *is* the One through whom all things are made. Visible in the person of Jesus of Nazareth in history, one and the same Logos remains present in creation today. Catholics cannot be indifferent to this *preambula fidei*, this preamble to the faith, writ-large that is the natural world, because we are not indifferent to the Word of whom it speaks. The task, as the priest-theologian Jean Mouroux once put it, is to integrate within the spiritual life what is already one in reality. The Logos of creation *is* the Logos made flesh; to sever one's self from the splendor of the cosmos is to be cut off from the Christ of whom it speaks.

·❈·

ACKNOWLEDGMENTS

SOMEWHERE in the pine barrens of Wisconsin, on an otherwise ordinary evening in late fall, the sandhill cranes came in by the thousands. Descending under the impulse power of the angels, their rosy underbellies bore the evening's blush of orange and purple hues, and, just for a moment, the natural law was made clear to me. Since that evening, now more than a decade old in my imagination, I have worked to develop the insights given there and have had the privilege of working through these ideas in a number of venues, academic and public.

Special gratitude needs to be given to The Saint Paul Seminary School of Divinity, especially Monsignor Aloysius Callaghan, Rector, for supporting my work and the work of The Center for Theological Formation. The many conferences and gatherings sponsored by the Center have served to strengthen the claims developed in this book. Special mention also needs to be given to Catholic Rural Life, especially Archbishop Paul Etienne, Chairman of the Board, and James Ennis, Executive Director. Their support and friendship has been an extraordinary blessing over the years. The faculty of the Center for Catholic Studies at the University of St. Thomas in St. Paul have also been a support, and The Chapelstone Foundation has been a long-time source of inspiration.

Portions of this more extended meditation were initially developed elsewhere: "In the Temple of Creation," a presentation given in 2011 at the International Congress convened by the Pontifical Council for Justice and Peace on the occasion of 50th Anniversary of *Mater et magistra*; "Beholding the Logos: The Church, the Environment and the Meaning of Man," in *Logos: A Journal of Catholic Thought and Culture* (2009); "Perennial Wisdom: Notes Toward a Green Thomism," in *Nova et Vetera* (2012); "'*Laudato Si*' and the Rise of Green Thomism," in *Nova et Vetera* (2016); and "The Place of Faith in the Geography of Hope," in *On Earth As It Is In Heaven: Cultivating a Contemporary Theology of Creation* (Eerdmans, 2016). I have also been especially blessed to explore in the United States and abroad these ideas through many conferences and colloquia sponsored by Catholic Rural Life and the International Catholic Rural Association. The many priests, theologians, philosophers, ecologists, students, poets, and farmers I have met over the years have shaped my thinking irrevocably. Fr. David Meconi, S.J., Fr. Andrew Brinkman, Vincenzo Conso, Anthony Granado, Tim Herrman, Sam Crane, Beth Ryan, Nancy Sannerud, Mary Byrne, and Sarah Spangenberg deserve special mention.

Finally, I owe my wife, Mary, a debt of gratitude—for just about everything, including this project. All the while meandering across the central United States, she has been the companion and mentor without whom nothing but the errors of my ways would be evident. Her encouragement, together with that of my three children Margaret, Ann, and Peter, and the hundreds of students over the years, has been a constant source of support.

·✦·

"Rather than a problem to be solved, the world is a joyful mystery to be contemplated with praise."[1]

WHEN St. Paul stepped into the Areopagus to call out the Athenians for their misguided religious practices and proclaimed the good news of Jesus Christ, he first appealed to a common ground of shared conviction: "The God who made the world and everything in it, being Lord of heaven and earth" (Acts 17:24). Paul established his authority among the crowds that day by affirming the common conviction that the world has a maker and its order rests in God. From this shared foundation he moves on to announce further claims: how the same God who has fashioned this heaven and the earth has also fashioned the peoples among its inhabitants; how "they should seek God, in the hope that they might feel after him and find him" (Acts 17:27); how this God is not far from each one of us; and how this God has acted decisively in the person of Jesus Christ by raising Him from the dead. While Paul is quickly dismissed by many in the crowd, "some men joined him and believed . . ." (Acts 17:34). And thus the good news of the Incarnation took root in the hearts

---

[1] Pope Francis, Encyclical Letter on Care for Our Common Home *Laudato si'* (May 24, 2015) (Vatican City: Libreria Editrice Vaticana, 2015), hereafter cited in text as *LS*.

of men and women: upon the common ground of a belief in a beautiful cosmos the new seed of Christ and His Church was planted.

This same path—from a consideration of the created universe to Christ—is available to us today. Until we recover the splendor of creation, the path to a vibrant Catholic culture seems cut off, and it is the special tragedy of this generation that many in the Church have held nature at arm's length. Until the promulgation of *Laudato si'*, the environment was not a primary matter of concern for the vast majority of Catholics, and even now some reports suggest that the Holy Father's encyclical has had limited impact, especially among self-described "conservative" Catholics.[2]

But such an antipathy to nature, or the environment, is alien to faith—and represents a distortion among the faithful that needs to be challenged and overcome. The ground, if you will, the setting in which effective evangelization occurs, must emerge from the fundamental conviction that the experience of the cosmos points to the existence of a God. Nature, faith teaches, is one of the first tutors in faith, and to hold creation in contempt or indifference is to slight the God from whom all good things come. Christians preach that the God of Jesus Christ *is* the God who has made all things. It was a central conviction of the earliest Christians; it is a vital conviction today.

---

[2] Nan Li et al., "Cross-pressuring conservative Catholics? Effects of Pope Francis' encyclical on the U.S. public opinion on climate change," *Climatic Change* 139, no. 3 (2016): 367–380, doi:10.1007/s10584-016-1821-z.

Such a claim about the cosmos and our place within it, however, whether framed in the language of "nature," or "the environment," or "creation," has in some important ways become increasingly toxic and thus makes the reality of a grace-filled, genuinely Catholic community that much more challenging to establish. Ironically, in this era of unprecedented abundance and ability, the human person is bereft of a sense of being at home in a universe in which the Logos is known and loved. Having circumscribed the globe and pierced the skies, our sense of place is increasingly tenuous. Well versed in the fragility of existence, we no longer readily turn to God at the heart of it all. Before the abyss of a starry sky or an expansive vista, we might be inspired to pray, but too often we quickly translate the urge into some remnant of our upbringing no longer to be taken seriously, or—even if a believer—will attribute the movement of faith to a personal style or preference. What we will not do, I think it is fair to say, is attribute the urge to pray to intelligence.

But the Church says otherwise: beneath the black-blue quilt of a starry night the urge to pray is irrepressible because prayer is the most intelligent response to the splendor of things. The new evangelization will effectively unfold when the natural instinct to worship is unleashed, when the splendor of things is passionately celebrated and announced. The Gospel will be renewed when God's first book, creation, is reopened and proclaimed again.

At the macro level, Enlightenment philosophies of nature have collectively created an intellectual climate in which nature no longer readily declares the glory of God. The rise of scientific materialism, itself a child of philosophical movements, has inclined the average person to believe that they are, as Myles Connolly puts it in the novel *Mr. Blue*, "bacteria breeding on a pebble in space or glints of ideas in a whirling void of abstractions."[3]

The body, too, as the hinge between heaven and earth, has lost its sacred character, its capacity to point to something more than itself. The last casualty in the war against things, the human body has become the mere place where "I" happen to hang out, the accidental occasion of my presence to another. Some now speak of the body as the medium through which I give myself, a "total gift of self," and rightly so. But few seem to speak any longer of the body in its originative, classic context: as the exclusive medium through which the human soul comes to know— dare I say it—splendid things.

And not just any things, but "the dearest freshness deep down things," as the priest poet Gerard Manley Hopkins puts it.[4] The glorious world of created being! The first tutors in the faith! This is the first book to be proclaimed; the Gospel His second. It is not just any Word-made-flesh that redeems, but the Word "without [whom] was not anything made that was made" (see Jn 1:3). It is the world in its radiance that provides the first encounter with the Word. The aim of this book is to recover something of the joyful mystery of creation, and put forward for reconsideration certain elements of the thought of St. Thomas Aquinas as an able guide in these challenging

---

[3] Myles Connolly, *Mr. Blue* (New York: Cluny Media, 2015), 34.
[4] "God's Grandeur," in Gerard Manley Hopkins, *Poems and Prose*, ed. W. H. Gardner (London: Penguin Classics, 1985), 27.

times when the search for an integral ecology is essential.

Chapter 1 begins with my experience of encountering a remarkable ignorance about our natural surroundings among otherwise highly educated and talented individuals. Students and peers alike seemed to succumb over the years to what some have called a "nature-deficit disorder," as if the issues of the environment and ecology were somehow not proper material for serious Catholics to consider, and that to take the environment too seriously showed a lack of formation or decorum, a faint and fawning sentimentality over things that ought not to occupy us. But such a detour from nature, however, is catastrophic for Catholic culture and ends up placing us in a rather alien position *vis-à-vis* the cosmos which is our home.

Chapter 2 fills in the intellectual gaps more fully and begins to provide the outlines of an ecology consistent with a Catholic vision of things. Regard for creation and its creatures has been a perennial part of Christian spirituality for centuries and in more recent decades has been the special concern of Catholic social teaching. In the United States in particular, the bishops have developed an extensive body of material discussing environmental and ecological issues, especially as they relate to agriculture and agricultural communities. The gap in our present knowledge is only further highlighted when seen against the extensive efforts put forth on the part of the magisterium to address ecological issues. I argue that the Church's social engagement, if it is to be recovered, needs to rediscover its Thomistic (meaning, related to Thomas Aquinas) roots. In particular, it was the loss of a common worldview supported by Thomistic philosophy which contributed to the increasing irrelevance of environmental issues and concerns in Catholic intellectual circles. By way of a remedy, the outlines of "Green Thomism" are put forward in this chapter; that is, a basic account, drawn from the insights of Thomistic philosophy and theology. The aim is to place ecology (the study and care of living organisms and their surroundings) where it belongs: at the forefront of Catholic concerns.

Chapter 3 focuses on the experience of awe before the beauty of creation—an experience to which almost everyone can relate. The beauty of creation is one of the first tutors in the faith and points us to the reality of God and His presence in a compelling way. Creation is God's first book and recovering the ability to read it is central in developing an integral ecology for future generations of faithful and committed alike. Drawing upon our experience of the beauty of nature only further strengthens the connections with ecology and our theological and spiritual tradition.

Chapter 4 briefly turns the reader's attention to *Laudato si'*, the groundbreaking encyclical written by Pope Francis in 2015, and sets this newest teaching of the Church within a deeper framework of St. Thomas' discussion of natural law. *Laudato si'* is in many ways innovative and creative in its tone and vision; at the same time it simply reaffirms the perennial claims about the meaning of creation and our place within it. By the end of Chapter IV, one can see more clearly a thread of teaching in the Church over the centuries up through the present papacy and can gain some confidence that there are invaluable resources in the Catholic theological tradition, especially from St. Thomas, that can contribute to the vital discussion of ecology and our responsibilities to care for the earth and each other.

Chapters 5, 6, and 7 focus attention on St. Thomas' discussion of the human person in light of original sin and its implications for us as embodied creatures within a divinely arranged cosmos. Gaining confidence in understanding the broader theological context more clearly in the imagination, I argue, will go a long way in securing a better grasp of the issues facing us when it comes to caring for the earth and each other. These are among the more technical aspects of the conversation, but they yield much fruit in establishing a responsible outlook on the duty to care for our common home, the earth.

Chapters 8 and 9 step back from the more technical elements and breathe in the winsome air of faith, prayer, and contemplation before creation. They point us in the direction of the center of our faith: the Eucharist. My aim in this chapter is that you not only think differently, and more faithfully, about the issues of the Church and ecology, but that you begin to pray differently, too, and in your Eucharistic practice you begin to see the integration of life and worship.

Each of the chapters concludes with selected passages which are intended to complement the content. Sometimes they directly affirm what is written. Other times they share the same tangent. Teachers and students can turn to them as prompts for further reflection and see in them occasions for further wonder and meditation.

Finally, in many ways this book assumes a familiarity with the thought of St. Thomas on some basic points, but

I have tried to write it in such a way that even the novice can find a point of entry into the conversation. Thankfully, there are many resources available through the web, especially materials supplied by Dominican communities, to aid in one's further learning. This is not an introduction to Thomism and even less an introduction to ecology. "Invitation" is a better term. It is my hope that you find in these field notes an invitation to enter more deeply into Thomism and ecology and in light of them, come to discover the Christ who is known and loved through both.

·⟐·

CHAPTER ONE

A Troubling Naiveté

"As Kingfishers catch fire, dragonflies draw flame
as tumbled over rim in roundy wells stones
ring . . ."[1]

"What's a Kingfisher?" she interjected.
We had just finished a first pass through Hopkins'
poem when the question came from the back of the class.
I explained that it was a bird often found perched on
branches overhanging still waters. "The bird rests perfectly still until it swoops down to capture an unsuspect-
ing fish," I said, "like something bursting into flames or
catching fire, catching glints of sunlight, in other words
. . . as kingfishers catch fire." The next day we took up
another Hopkins poem, "Binsey Poplars." It was about a
grove of poplar trees that had been cut down. And another
question came up: "What's a poplar tree?" I paused and
tried to explain.

---

[1] "As Kingfishers Catch Fire," in Gerard Manley Hopkins, *Poems and
Prose*, ed. W. H. Gardner (London: Penguin Classics, 1985), 51.

The Jesuit priest poet, Gerard Manley Hopkins, S.J., penned his poems at the end of the nineteenth century, when his beloved English countryside, a world that gave such glory to his God, was becoming increasingly marred by industrialization. The loss of the beauty of creation, the silencing of creation's voice, was often one of his central themes. Hopkins went on to write several poems celebrating the earth—"charged with the glory of God"—and his poetry speaks beautifully about the dignity of creation and our status as its stewards. He is one of the outstanding figures in the Catholic literary tradition. And it was in teaching his poetry to my students that my interest in the issue of an integral ecology began.

It was not too long before I started to notice even among very bright students a significant gap in their knowledge about what I took to be some of the most basic features of the natural world around us. Friends and colleagues, too, seemed strikingly unaware of their natural circumstances, often being caught off guard by what in many ways are the basic elements of a natural intelligence. I was once asked by someone curious about the rain barrels at the base of the gutters, "Is it safe to put rainwater on the garden?" "Well, God does," I said, "so I think so." And to this day I smile when I recall the question I was asked by a college graduate: "So what does the artichoke animal look like?" The recipe had called for "artichoke hearts," and so the question seemed natural enough.

We've all experienced it in ourselves, too: an astonishing ignorance about natural surroundings and the environment. Richard Louv calls it a "nature-deficit disorder" and it is often a good lesson in humility and the occasion of due laughter.[2] But on a broader and more systemic scale, ignorance of the natural world is costly, not only in terms of the ability to care for the earth in thoughtful ways, but spiritually, too. Ignorance of creation is ignorance of the Creator and the increasing failure to read the book of nature undermines the capacity to live a life in grace. Catholicism, it will be said repeatedly in these pages, celebrates the Logos made flesh—the very same Logos through whom all things are sustained in their existence. We are not indifferent to the world through which the Word speaks.

And so I thought I would try to address this "nature-deficit" in my class and, in my own naiveté, decided to go out into the rural areas of Minnesota to try to begin to expose students to the great surroundings of the Central Midwest. We went to three different farms: a large industrial operation, a much more modestly-scaled farm, and a hobby farm. At the end of this little retreat, I asked the students to write comments about their experience: what they learned, what worked, and what didn't. A student wrote: "I appreciated the weekend because I didn't know they raised animals in Minnesota."

In her defense you perhaps need to know that she was from California—Los Angeles, to be exact—and flew from LA to the Twin Cities and back at the beginning and end of the school year. If you were familiar with the drive from the airport to my campus in Saint Paul, you would know that you pass through some of the most beautiful

<hr/>

[2] Richard Louv, *Last Child in the Woods: Saving Our Children from Nature-Deficit Disorder* (Chapel Hill, NC: Algonquin Books of Chapel Hill, 2005).

neighborhoods and cruise along well maintained city parks that flank the picturesque banks of the Mississippi. It is no wonder, then, that she would have no idea that animals were raised in Minnesota. There were no animals to be seen, except for pets and a few squirrels; no farms or farm lands in sight; no processing plants or food workers, just the magical world of upscale private school living, where food appears on shelves in abundance and "nature" is a mere tagline on some wholesome product at the local co-op.

Of course we can smile about our naiveté. Each of us can claim a similar lack of awareness at times and laugh at our occasional ignorance. But this exchange was something of a wake-up call for me. What I was coming to experience was something much broader and widespread. The "nature-deficit" that Richard Louv writes about was more than simply an occasional ignorance. No. It seemed as if our ignorance of nature was almost willed, a kind of intentional stance one took toward the earth and its surroundings. We were not merely lacking in knowledge; it was as if we were determined not to know. "Nature" was the concern of "them"—environmentalists, liberals especially—and serious Catholics didn't regard the earth and its creatures. As Pope Francis puts it in *Laudato si'*, care for the environment was something "only the faint-hearted care about" (*LS*, no. 116). My students' ignorance, in other words, was not the exception. In fact, ignorance of the natural world seemed to be the new normal.

About ten years ago, I had the privilege of participating in an international conference sponsored by one of the pontifical councils. I was delighted by the invitation but remember especially a phrase from the letter: "Because of your expertise in the United States and Canada . . ." Poor Canada, I thought. Surely, this exaggeration was just a matter of courteous encouragement for my work and additional enticement to attend. Surely, an entire team of Catholic institutions across North America had taken up the issues of agriculture from the perspective of Catholic social teaching. After all, this was the United States (and Canada); agriculture is a dominant industry—a $400-billion-dollar-a-year industry. Surely, the issues were being thoroughly engaged and discussed as Catholic academia is apt to do.

Moreover, I recalled the privilege of joining together with several hundred thousand people at Living History Farms in 1979 and participating in the memorable liturgy of St. John Paul II, celebrated in the open fields of rural Iowa. I also came to know that John Paul II's visit was just one piece of a long continuum of pastoral efforts on the part of the Church in the United States to engage the issues of agriculture.

I knew that both at the national and regional levels the US Bishops had been putting forward a considerable effort to lead the Church to a deeper consideration of the human, ethical, and social concerns which lie at the heart of the ecological tradition, especially American agricultural life.[3] I was also increasingly aware of the extensive work of

---

[3] A sampling of teachings from the US Bishops include: (2003) *For I Was Hungry and You Gave Me Food: Catholic Reflections on Food, Farmers, and Farmworkers*; (1991) *Renewing the Earth: An Invitation to Reflection and Action on Environment in Light of Catholic Social Teaching*; (1988) *Report of the Ad Hoc Task Force on Food, Agriculture, and Rural Concerns*; (1986) *Economic Justice for All: A Pastoral Letter on Catholic Social Teaching and the U.S. Economy*; (1975) *Food Policy and the Church: Specific Proposals*; (1974) *Statement on the World Food Crisis: A*

the National Catholic Rural Life Conference (now called Catholic Rural Life) which for over eighty years worked to bring the Gospel of Jesus Christ and the social teachings of His Church into the heart of rural life in the United States. Established by Fr. (later Archbishop) Edwin O'Hara in 1923, the Conference continues to be one of the principle means by which Catholic social thought is promulgated among rural farmers of the United States.[4]

I knew that at its peak Catholic Rural Life and its affiliates sponsored some 60 schools of rural instruction and philosophy, enrolling 1,700 priests, 9,000 women religious, and 12,000 laity. Its annual rural life gathering attracted 15,000 participants at its 1941 gathering in Bismarck, North Dakota![5] Surely all of these collective efforts made a lasting impression on the fields of education and the leadership in Catholic intellectual circles.

And then it was my turn for astonishing ignorance. I discovered a fact that gave inspiration to this project: of the 244 Catholic universities in the United States, not a single one offers a program of study in agriculture. Not one! My student would never have known they raised animals in Minnesota, because no one in Catholic higher education in Minnesota—or the United States for that

---

Pastoral Plan of Action; (1973) *Resolution on Farm Labor*; (1972) *Where Shall the People Live?*; (1968) *Statement on Farm Labor*; (1958) *Explosion or Backfire?*

[4] For a life of Archbishop O'Hara, see Timothy Michael Dolan, *Some Seed Fell on Good Ground: The Life of Edwin V. O'Hara* (Washington, DC: Catholic University of America Press, 1992).

[5] David Bovée, *The Church & The Land: The National Catholic Rural Life Conference and American Society, 1923–2007* (Washington, DC: Catholic University of America Press, 2010), 140.

matter—seems to think it is worth knowing. Her innocence was not mere naiveté; our innocence was not something quaint, something to be smiled at in some moment
of self-awareness. Our "innocence" was, in fact, an indica-
tor—the symptom of a deeper cultural blind spot, a feature of a much larger indifference to creation and its care.
That I was, in fact, considered an international expert on
the matter was so much more distressing than edifying.

Happily, in 2015, Pope Francis took this issue head-
on and wrote a groundbreaking encyclical, *Laudato si'*,
designed to raise awareness of not just agriculture and
its neglect, but of broader cultural indifference to issues
of ecology at large. The subject of intense scrutiny and
highly controversial in its release, the encyclical called all
Catholics, indeed all global citizens, to reexamine their
attitudes toward all of creation and bring about in their
lives an ecological conversion of heart.

The Holy Father confirmed what many had experienced: that something is deeply flawed in attitudes toward
creation and that a *metanoia*, a change of heart, is called
for if we are to combat its cumulative effects, now evident
in widespread ecological challenges, especially climate
change. Pope Francis calls all of us to a deeper examina-
tion of conscience regarding the place of human beings
within the created cosmos.

From my limited vantage, the encyclical could not
come soon enough, and this book is intended to inspire
an intellectual and spiritual renewal consonant with his
vision for an ecological conversion. Whether we call it a
nature-deficit, a simple naiveté, or a cultural blind spot,
Laudato si' teaches us that such ignorance is alien to the

Catholic faith and spiritual life the Church seeks to nourish. Ignorance of the natural environment can no longer be seen as benign innocence. It is a sin of omission and requires a conversion, an ecological conversion. Each one of us is called to develop an integral ecology, an integral spirituality, one that seeks to take seriously our place on this earth and the vocation to be His stewards.

Despite the global efforts to raise awareness around the issues of environmental stewardship, ecological responsibility, and an appropriate spirituality of care for the earth and its creatures, many still have difficulty coming to terms with Pope Francis' "new vision" of the earth and our vocation as its stewards. The Holy Father has been denounced as an innovator by many, accused of inserting into the Catholic theological tradition a mere transitory opinion on the meaning and value of the earth and our role.

Ecology often attracts spontaneous negative reactions within large segments of the general population and not a few segments within the Catholic community. Resistance to developing an ecologically sensitive spirituality is particularly vexing, even painful, when seen from the vantage of the historic pastoral efforts especially here in the United States.

But we cannot afford to have another generation of otherwise bright young people wondering if animals are raised in Minnesota. And this is not because we may be on the brink of an ecological catastrophe from which we may never fully recover. That is a matter better left to scientists, prognosticators, and those with a penchant for the apocalyptic. No. An ecological conversion is called for *because* of our Catholic faith, not in spite of it. A widespread rethinking of attitudes and practices is demanded. I refuse to yield this body to its earth without having done all I can, with the help of His grace, to give glory and honor to the One who has fashioned us all.

Green Thomism is a neologism coined to express the retrieval of St. Thomas' vision of creation and the unique vocation of human beings within it, in order to inspire a more robust spiritual life with integral ecology at its core.[6] The effort is neither historical in its methodology nor comprehensive in its expectation. My aim is more limited, but no less important: to inspire a conversation among disparate parties that for too long have kept each other at arm's length. Thomists (followers of St. Thomas Aquinas) could profit from the engagement of modern cultural movements such as the rise of environmental concern, and environmentalists (ecologists and organic consumers included) could benefit from a deeper reflection on the implications and impact of their decisions regarding life on

---

[6] A sample of others who have sought to integrate these issues include: Willis Jenkins, "Biodiversity and Salvation: Thomistic Roots for Environmental Ethics," *The Journal of Religion* 83, no. 3 (July 2003): 401–420; Willis Jenkins, *Ecologies of Grace: Environmental Ethics and Christian Theology* (New York: Oxford University Press, 2008); Fr. Robert Grant, *A Case Study in Thomistic Environmental Ethics: The Ecological Crisis in the Loess Hills of Iowa* (Lewiston, NY: The Edwin Mellen Press, 2007); Jill LeBlanc, "Eco-Thomism," *Environmental Ethics* 21, no. 3 (Fall 1999): 293–306. For an opposing view see Francisco Benzoni, "Thomas Aquinas and Environmental Ethics: A Reconsideration of Providence and Salvation," *The Journal of Religion* 85, no. 3 (July 2005): 446–476; Francisco Benzoni, *Ecological Ethics and the Human Soul: Aquinas, Whitehead, and the Metaphysics of Value* (Notre Dame: University of Notre Dame Press, 2007). For an engaging critique of the latter, see Christopher Brown's review at *Notre Dame Philosophical Reviews*, online at http://ndpr.nd.edu/review.cfm?id=13765.

this beautiful earth. Coming together in a spirit of mutual sympathy and understanding, together they can provide the much-needed catalyst for a reinvigoration of culture, both Catholic and otherwise.

More specifically, Thomism supplies the intellectual wherewithal that moves the Catholic imagination beyond sentimentality. Catholic social teaching is often described as "the best kept secret of the Church." It will remain so until the intellectual foundations upon which so much of it depends are more robustly explored and defended in institutions of higher learning. The philosophical framework supplied by St. Thomas regarding "the nature of nature" and the vision of the human person as a union of both material and spiritual principles can provide the necessary components of an integral ecology that is more than the expression of a private fancy or a program of public manipulation. It can be the catalyst to situate the newest insights of ecological and environmental science within the ancient and vital conversation of the Church.

From the beginning, we have to recognize that much of Thomas' thought is embedded in the medieval theories of causality that are no longer tenable in the light of contemporary science. His discussion of the status of creatures in the eschaton, the end of the world, seems especially hampered by his thinking concerning the nature and influence of celestial spheres.[7] As a Church, we seem to be developing a richer, more inclusive notion of the

---

[7] For a detailed discussion of the relationships among the heavenly bodies and lower creatures, especially in the eschaton, see Thomas Aquinas' *De potentia* 5, 5–10.

new creation than Thomas would have allowed, and we can look forward to a more comprehensive vision of the new heavens and earth promised in Revelation. We serve neither the Church nor the legacy of St. Thomas by merely repeating his thought. Rather, we serve the Tradition and honor his legacy by continuing to enter more deeply into the treasury of wisdom it is intended to hand on.

We also have to leapfrog over the postconciliar squabbles which have reduced much of contemporary Catholic intellectual life to an intramural parlor game, and learn, once again, that faith creates culture, culture shapes people, and people shape the earth. Integral ecology of the Green Thomist variety moves back and forth within this circuit, from adoration of the Triune God to the minutest concern for the merest of animacules occupying the tiniest of habitats on some rarest corner of the earth—and back again. The urgency of the task is not driven, at least on my part, by an anxious concern about the future of the earth and its inhabitants. Instead it is driven by the deepest desire to contribute to those conditions in which Christ is passionately loved and served in the furthest reaches of His universe. Green Thomists live in the utter confidence that the love of God, poured into hearts by the Holy Spirit, is meant to illumine every nook and cranny of each human psyche, every crag and crown of each fragment of the universe; with Thomas we affirm that nothing means nothing to God.

SELECTED READINGS FOR CHAPTER ONE

On the World as Created "In Wisdom"

We have to make evident once more what is meant by the world's having been created "in wisdom." . . . Only then can conscience and norm enter again into proper relationship. For then it will become clear that conscience is not some individualistic (or collective) calculation; rather it is a "con-sciens," a "knowing along with" creation and, through creation, with God the Creator. Then, too, it will be rediscovered that man's greatness does not lie in the miserable autonomy of proclaiming himself his one and only master, but in the fact that his being allows the highest wisdom, truth itself, to shine through. Then it will become clear that man is so much the greater the more he is capable of hearing the profound message of creation, the message of the Creator. And then it will be apparent how harmony with creation, whose wisdom becomes our norm, does not mean a limitation upon our freedom but is rather an expression of our reason and our dignity. Then the body also is given its due honor: it is no longer something "used," but is the temple of authentic human dignity because it is God's handiwork in the world. Then is the equal dignity of man and woman made manifest precisely in the fact that they are different. One will then begin to understand once again that their bodiliness reaches the metaphysical depths and is the basis of a symbolic metaphysics whose denial or neglect does not ennoble man but destroys him.

—Joseph Cardinal Ratzinger, "Fundamental Characteristics of the Present Crisis of Faith," in *L'Osservatore Romano*, July 24, 1989

On Thomas and the Acceptance
of Creatureliness

It is my conviction that Thomas Aquinas's teaching on creation is, at the same time, the most powerful and most overlooked dimension of his doctrine. When we attend to him carefully on this score we discover something marvelous and wholly unexpected: the basic energy of the created realm is a relationship of love. God continually pours out the gift of being, and the world is at every moment a sheer receptivity, an openness toward that gift. Human beings are in a privileged position because they are able to perceive and to celebrate this relationship that they are. Indeed, at the heart of the spiritual life, for Aquinas, is this struggle to see authentically who we are in relation to the God who perpetually offers us "newness of being." When we realize, in imitation of Christ, that we are "nothing" in the presence of the creating God, we become "everything," a full reflection of the divine glory. Sin is thus a sort of illusion, a stubborn clinging to falsehood, an insistence that we stand over and against God, the supreme being. Let go of yourself, implies Thomas, in an ecstatic acceptance of creatureliness, and you will find security that you so long for. In the face of your greatest fears, give yourself away.

—Robert Barron, *Thomas Aquinas: Spiritual Master* (New York, NY: The Crossroad Publishing Company, 2000), 138–139

On an Inadequate Notion of
Human Persons

Neglecting to monitor the harm done to nature and the environmental impact of our decisions is only the most striking sign of a disregard for the message contained in the structures of nature itself. When we fail to acknowledge as part of reality the worth of a poor person, a human embryo, a person with disabilities—to offer just a few examples—it becomes difficult to hear the cry of nature itself; everything is connected. Once the human being declares independence from reality and behaves with absolute dominion, the very foundations of our life begin to crumble, for "instead of carrying out his role as a cooperator with God in the work of creation, man sets himself up in place of God and thus ends up provoking a rebellion on the part of nature."

This situation has led to a constant schizophrenia, wherein a technocracy which sees no intrinsic value in lesser beings coexists with the other extreme, which sees no special value in human beings. But one cannot prescind from humanity. There can be no renewal of our relationship with nature without a renewal of humanity itself. There can be no ecology without an adequate anthropology. When the human person is considered as simply one being among others, the product of chance or physical determinism, then "our overall sense of responsibility wanes." A misguided anthropocentrism need not necessarily yield to "biocentrism," for that would entail adding yet another imbalance, failing to solve present problems and adding new ones. Human beings cannot be expected to feel responsibility for the world unless, at the same time, their unique capacities of knowledge, will, freedom and responsibility are recognized and valued.

—Pope Francis, *Laudato si'*, nos. 117–118

SELECTED RESOURCES FOR CHAPTER ONE
Robert Barron, *Thomas Aquinas: Spiritual Master* (New
York, NY: The Crossroad Publishing Company, 1996).
Mieczysław A. Krąpiec, O.P., *I—Man: An Outline of Phil-
osophical Anthropology*, trans. Marie Lescoe, Andrew
Woznicki, and Theresa Sandok, et. al. (New Britain,
CT: Mariel Publications, 1983).
Jean-Pierre Torrell, O.P., *Saint Thomas Aquinas: Volume
2: Spiritual Master*, trans. Robert Royal (Washington,
DC: The Catholic University of America Press, 2003).

·᭤·

CHAPTER TWO

THE OUTLINE OF RECOVERY

"Some hold that our views about creatures are irrelevant to the truth of the faith so long as our religious attitude is correct. They have adopted a thoroughly unsound position."[1]

THE history of the ecological movement within the Catholic Church is yet to be written, but when it is, one will discover that many of the practices now espoused by the most progressive minds were, in fact, voiced in a prior era by those Catholics engaged in the issues of ecological stewardship.[2] Buying locally sourced, sustainably raised

---

[1] Thomas Aquinas, *Summa Contra Gentiles* II, 3, (hereafter, *SCG*), cited in Thomas Gilby, O.P., *Philosophical Texts* (London: Oxford University Press, 1952), 29, (hereafter, Gilby).

[2] See for example Denis Fahey, C.S.Sp, *The Church and Farming* (Cork, IE: The Forum Press, 1953); Luigi Ligutti and John Rawe, *Rural Roads to Security* (Milwaukee, WI: The Bruce Publishing Company, 1940); George Speltz, *The Importance of Rural Life According to the Philosophy of Thomas Aquinas* (Eugene, OR: Wipf & Stock, 2003); National Catholic Rural Life Conference, *Manifesto on Rural Life* (Milwaukee, WI: The Bruce Publishing Company, 1939). Peruse vir-

foods from smaller scale family owned vendors was a consistent mantra of Catholic rural life for decades leading up to its now more popular expression in the broader culture. It is difficult to distinguish sometimes between the enthusiasms of the Catholic growers of the 1940s and the co-op movements present today.

Long before Aldo Leopold penned his classic *Sand County Almanac* in 1949 and launched the environmental movement,[3] before Sigurd Olson wrote *Listening Point* in 1958,[4] or Rachel Carson sounded the alarm in *Silent Spring* in 1962, before E. F. Schumacher drafted *Small is Beautiful* in 1973 and inspired a generation of thought on sustainable economics,[5] before Michael Pollan crafted *Second Nature* in 1991,[6] before Joel Salatin turned the first shovel of dirt on Polyface Farm,[7] before the Organic Consumers Association,[8] *Mother Earth News*, and the Slow Food Movement, there were extensive and consistent Catholic voices championing the importance of created nature and the imperative to steward it. The absence of

tually any volume of the National Catholic Rural Life Conference bulletins during its first few decades and one finds an astonishing sympathy between the views expressed there and some of the most recent advocates for an environmentally sensitive way of life.

[3] Aldo Leopold, *A Sand County Almanac*, 1949 (reprint, New York: Ballantine Books, 1990).

[4] Sigurd Olson, *Listening Point*, 1958 (reprint, Minneapolis, MN: University of Minnesota Press, 1997).

[5] E. F. Schumacher, *Small is Beautiful: Economics as if People Mattered* (New York: Harper Perennial, 1989).

[6] Michael Pollan, *Second Nature: A Gardener's Education* (New York: Grove Press, 1991).

[7] see http://www.polyfacefarms.com/

[8] see http://www.organicconsumers.org/

a serious account of these efforts is a curious lacuna in Catholic cultural scholarship. Let us hope that *Laudato si'* inspires a correction.

Laudato si' is hardly the first time that the Church has been called upon to confront widely held but alien visions of material creation and the place of humanity within it. In virtually every century since the beginning of the Church, ordinary saints and extraordinary scholars have followed the impulse of Sacred Scripture and contemplated the glorious universe in praise of the God who made it.[9] In the writings of Athanasius (d. 373), we read of creation pointing to the Creator; Ephrem the Syrian (d. 373) defends the "book of creation;" Basil of Caesaria (d. 379) expounds on the works of the Master Craftsman; John of Damascus (d. 749) speaks on the sacramentality of matter; and John Scotus Eriugena (d. 815) speaks of the presence of God in creation. Hugh of St. Victor (d. 1141) reflects on the sacramentality of creation, and Bernard of Clairvaux (d. 1153), Albert Magnus (d. 1280), and Bonaventure (d. 1274), to name only a few, all give witness to creation's power to disclose something of the reality of God.

In the fourth century especially, St. Augustine met the challenge of the Manichaean heresy, a bizarre amal-

---

[9] For a compelling reconstruction of much of the early Church's engagement with issues of environmental concern, see Jame Schaefer, *Theological Foundations for Environmental Ethics: Reconstructing Patristic & Medieval Theological Concepts* (Washington, DC: Georgetown University Press, 2009). For a broader survey of Western engagement with such related issues see Clarence Glacken, *Traces on the Rhodian Shore: Nature and Culture in Western Thought from Ancient Time to the End of the Eighteenth Century* (Berkeley, CA: University of California Press, 1976).

gam of fantastical claims about the origins of the universe and our place within it. While Manichaeism may not be described as an environmental philosophy without some charge of anachronism, it was nonetheless a comprehensive philosophy of nature and human life. Not unlike present circumstances, the Church found itself needing to offer a defense of the goodness of all creatures, human and otherwise, giving comfort to an anxious world searching amidst what they were convinced was a cosmos destined for annihilation.

The Albigensian heresy of the twelfth century (itself a prodigy of Manichaeism) was still another "environmental philosophy," one that endorsed a vision of material creation as utterly corrupted and the human person as an abomination within it. Through the inspiration of St. Dominic, the Order of Preachers was founded in part to confront these concerns. The most famous of its members, Thomas Aquinas, joined the order in April of 1244 and committed his life to an intense study of the Christian faith. His unparalleled genius and personal holiness testified to his saintliness, but perhaps more importantly for today, he defended a vision of the created order that can still supply the necessary tools to address the question of the environment and our place within it.

The point of these brief remarks is to underscore that Pope Francis could draw upon the universal Church in his drafting of *Laudato si'* because the foundations for a theology of creation and its implications for the care of the earth had already been laid throughout the centuries of the Church's collective discernment. It is unfortunate that so many Catholics, especially in the United States, fail to recognize the Church's tradition reflected in Francis' efforts.

A few scholars have openly wondered why ecological concerns have gone largely unattended in the average American Catholic's experience despite the once-successful efforts in the Church's systemic social engagement, especially in the arena of agriculture. Christopher Hamlin and John T. McGreevy, in "The Greening of America, Catholic Style, 1930–1950," chronicle the rise and fall of the "green revolution" advocated by the Church in America.[10] They are among the few in contemporary Catholic intellectual circles who seemed to have noticed that there was, in fact, a robust effort on the part of many to bring Catholic intellectual tradition, specifically the social tradition, to bear upon the circumstances of Catholic agrarian life.[11]

They point to a number of causes that signaled the waning of the Church's influence in ecological matters, and in the end they do not mince words. "Not only did the [Church's] green revolution fail to take off, it left hardly a memorial of its failure."[12] While it is impressive to read their rather extensive survey of the various elements of the movement in its heyday, the gem of their remarks appears

[10] Christopher Hamlin and John T. McGreevy, "The Greening of America, Catholic Style, 1930–1950," *Environmental History* 11, no. 3 (July 2006): 464–499.

[11] Michael J. Woods, S.J., *Cultivating the Soil and Soul: Twentieth-Century Catholic Agrarians Embrace the Liturgical Movement* (Collegeville, MN: Liturgical Press, 2010).

[12] Christopher Hamlin and John T. McGreevy, in "The Greening of America, Catholic Style, 1930–1950," *Environmental History*, vol. 11, no. 3 (July 2006): 486.

in the penultimate sentence of the essay: "Recognition of a longer history of Catholic . . . engagement with the issues of environmental quality can perhaps do something to challenge the image of religious environmentalism as an afterthought rather than as an essential component of a cosmology (as Thomas Aquinas certainly recognized and most anthropologists would acknowledge.)"[13]

There you have it: the central tenet of the green revolution "Catholic style." The revolution was rooted in the philosophy of creation, what they call "cosmology," of St. Thomas Aquinas. In other words, the Church was enabled to address critical issues of ecological practices because the Church was invested, deeply invested through the centuries, in a dominant philosophy of creation, of creatures and their habitats, including the human person, who participates in that same cosmic order.

The demise of any social traction regarding the Church and ecology, then, was due in large part to the collapse of the philosophical foundations regarding creation and creatures upon which that social agenda depended—and still depends to this day, up to and including the historic pronouncement of *Laudato si'*. That foundation (it cannot be emphasized enough) was established, maintained, and developed along Thomistic categories, and it was this intellectual tradition that sustained the conversations through most of the modern period. Recovering that Thomistic nomenclature—its philosophical, ethical, and theological vision of creation—will be the first and crucial step in developing a coherent spiritual set of practices and an ecologically converted life

---

[13] Ibid., 489.

that gives witness to integral ecology today.

A Green Thomism needs to be fostered throughout Catholic intellectual and socially-minded communities. For not only would a renewed and robust vision of the created order animate our engagement with the newest ecological concerns, but it would also extend the reach of our intellectual tradition beyond the horizon of punditry and pronouncements. Absent a coherent, philosophically integrated worldview of creation and its creatures, even the best moments of magisterial instruction simply dissipate into the rhetoric of the times. The good seed falls on poor soil because the people are unprepared to nurture and sustain what has been given them.

Inspired by St. Thomas, Green Thomists insist, among other things, that the human person is an embodied, spiritual creature dwelling in a cosmos of created natures, intelligently ordered by God and capable of being intelligibly grasped by human reason; they insist that this wisdom of creation is something prior to us, given by God and discovered through intelligence; and they insist that despite original sin, the original wisdom of the Creator still permeates creation and provides norms for its care as well as human flourishing.

THE HUMAN PERSON

According to St. Thomas, the human being is an *embodied* intellectual being and as such occupies the lowest order of intellectual creatures. Notwithstanding its dignity as the only creature in the material universe that bears the image of God, the human being is dependent upon organic substances in order to engage in any intellectual acts. Thomas' portrait of the person is premised upon the notion that human knowing is dependent upon things, *things already thick with meaning*, immersed in light, pregnant with intelligence.

It is popular to imagine the search for wisdom with the image of a person holding a lighted candle in an otherwise dark abyss. There the inquirer goes, holding firmly to the light, searching for purported wisdom amidst the darkness of the universe. For St. Thomas and the tradition he inspired, however, the situation is precisely the opposite. It is the created things that are permeated with light and I, with my limited intellectual powers, am the one who suffers a kind of glaucoma.

Blinded before the brilliance of things, I am an apprentice in the braille of all learning. I feel my way across the texts of the world, discerning through its impressions the message of creation, the message of the Creator. Largely deaf to its vocation, I listen in solitude, for as the author of Job prompts us: "ask the beasts, and they will teach you; the birds of the air, and they will tell you; or the plants of the earth, and they will teach you; and the fish of the sea will declare to you. Who among all these does not know that the hand of the LORD has done this?" (Job 12:7–9, *The New Oxford Annotated Bible*).

The human person is not tossed into a darkened abyss of space beyond space, abandoned to flail in a sea of endless absurdity; every human person is born amidst a universe of brilliant diamonds, a world so radiant with light their brightness causes one to wince and thus see only in the most diffuse of contexts. Because intelligible things emerge prior to one's knowing, because one can understand only what is already all ready to be understood, one enters a world filled with the giftedness of creatures already formed, an apprentice in the jeweler's shop owned by the heavenly Father. "Rather than a problem to be solved," Francis tells us, "the world is a joyful mystery to be contemplated with gladness and praise."[14]

THE CREATED ORDER

Green Thomism asserts that divine wisdom speaks through things. The coherence of living organisms as well as the community toward which they naturally tend are objectively given in reality and express "a design of love and truth" of the Creator Himself.[15] Such an order "is prior to us and has been given to us by God as the setting of our life."[16] It is not contrived from a set of clear and distinct ideas of some disembodied cogito; it is not the projection of a transcendental ego; nor is it the remnant of some human habit or social custom. Wisdom is intrinsic to things and its apprehension by reason is an exercise in objective knowing.[17]

---

[14] *LS*, no. 12

[15] Benedict XVI, Encyclical Letter on Charity in Truth, *Caritas in veritate* (June 29, 2009), no. 48.

[16] Ibid.

[17] "The first act of the intellect is to know, not its own action, not the ego, not phenomena, but objective and intelligible being." Reginald Garrigou-Lagrange, O.P., *Reality: A Synthesis of Thomistic Thought*, trans. Patrick Cummins, O.S.B. (St. Louis: Herder, 1950), 388. Cf. Thomas Aquinas, *Summa Theologiae* I 84.7: "The proper object of the human intellect, which is united to a body is a quiddity or nature existing in corporeal matter; and through such natures of visible things it rises to a certain knowledge of things invisible." Unless otherwise indicated, all citations of the *Summa Theologiae* will be taken from Thomas Aquinas, *Summa Theologiae* (Allen, TX: Christian Classics, 1981), hereafter *ST*.

The entire hierarchy of being, from the lowliest creature up to God, is permeated by a provident intelligence that supplies the necessary connections between lower creation and its grace-filled care. Every creature participates in this eternal law of God's creative action, and the rational creature's participation is held in special esteem. Thomas calls human participation in this universe of meaning in motion the natural law.

Integral ecology, in this context, is an *ars cooperativa*, a "co-operative art," because its demands are ineluctably aligned with the intelligible forces of nature itself. In that manner, it is not unlike the teacher who guides the natural desire to know on the part of the student, or the doctor who capitalizes on the natural desire to live. The ecologically minded farmer, too, labors with nature's creative forces and coaxes from the earth the fruits she is destined by providence to yield. The art of agriculture was distinct from that of the sculptor, for example, who works to create what is first only in the mind of the artist. Instead one speaks of crop "yield" and animal "husbandry," pointing to the fundamentally collaborative status of the farmer before the earth. The prudent steward enacts the natural law, not as some despot over an untamed wilderness, nor as a demagogue over an otherwise meaningless order of things. The prudent human being inhabits a provident order, as one who bears the image of God amidst the traces of God, as a steward in the temple of creation.

In such a setting, the human person is not taken to be the exception to an otherwise purely materialist order of things; rather, the human person is set amidst a radically intelligible order of creation already permeated with

organic creatures, specifically, the plant and animal kingdoms of lower creation. At the heart of a sound integral
ecology, then, lies a confidence in a natural philosophy
of creation, an order utterly dependent upon a provident
First Cause, whose causality extends to the operations
of individual creatures.[18] Against the vast and undiffer-
entiated universe of modernist materialist philosophy, a
distinctly Catholic approach to creation includes the distinctive and ordered aspects of each creature.[19]

In its secular mode, one can understand the increasing
emergence of environmental awareness as the unthematic
revolt of conscience among those descendants of the Enlightenment who intuit that something is deeply flawed
in the habit of treating nature as a mere raw datum of
purposeless matter. Green Thomism can contribute to the
renewal of an eco-realism by supplying not only a richer
notion of the person as the subject who stewards, but also a
richer notion of created things as objects to be stewarded.

THE IMPLICATIONS OF ORIGINAL SIN

Finally, Green Thomists argue that despite the devastating consequence of original sin, its disordering effects do
not permeate the "lower orders" of creation, that is, those
ranks of organic beings who lack the capacity for deliberate choosing. We will have to defer to a later section
of this book to explore this thesis more fully, but it is

---

[18] *ST* I 22.2

[19] Benedict XVI, *Caritas in veritate*, no. 48: "Reducing nature merely to
a collection of contingent data ends up doing violence to the environment and even encouraging activity that fails to respect human nature
itself."

perhaps relevant to point out here that it marks one of the most important elements in crafting a responsible integral ecology and a sound spiritual life.

In conclusion, it should be noted that many of these insights would have been familiar to the attentive student in Catholic colleges prior to the later 1960s, for many of these elements formed the essential outline of every student's intellectual formation.

In many of the curricula of Catholic universities up to the mid to late sixties, the general subject of the philosophy of nature was taken up early in one's program of study and was further divided into "cosmology" and "psychology," or a study of inanimate and animated creatures. (Natural theology, which treated the subject of God's existence, was considered a third dimension.) Together, these courses aimed at providing an account both of the human person, but also (and this was essential) an account of the created world as intelligently ordered by God. In other words, in the intellectual landscape of thought, the human person was always set within the broader framework of an intelligible order of things, the existence of which was sustained by God as both the First Cause and its end. The discussion of the unique character of the human soul and its rational powers, in other words, would have been presented only after an extended treatment of the other, more simple orders of creatures were explored.

The "green revolution" Catholic style and the extensive engagement with the social issues of the day, including ecology, would have been constructed upon an affirmation of this order of things and our fundamental responsibility within it. The green revolution was the social expression of a more comprehensive Green Thomism. Stewardship was an extension of cosmology.

Over time, with the decreasing presence of this kind of philosophy in Catholic undergraduate formation, philosophical psychology and philosophical cosmology disappeared from the tool kit of Catholics generally. The net result was something like we often find today. If there was a course that treats on the human person in a Catholic college curriculum, it was most likely the "philosophy of the human person," and dealt with debates on post-Cartesian terms; that is, extensive energy was spent considering (and defending) the notion of the person as a union of body and soul, a notion still so central to the Catholic view of the person. But this *"hylemorphic" or "matter-form"* account of the person was not strictly speaking a "philosophy of the human person."

It was, instead, the focused application of a more general philosophy of nature, in which every animated creature—plants, animals, and organisms—were understood to be "body/soul" composites, consistent with the philosophical tradition handed on through the centuries. In this worldview (called Aristotelian/Thomistic because of the influence of Aristotle and St. Thomas) the human person as a body/soul composite is less the odd exception to an order of reality that is otherwise mechanical/material/meaningless. Instead, the human person was considered within a menagerie of living bodies, other creatures within a divinely arranged cosmos. For every living creature—carrots, cucumbers, Cockatiels, and kings—was understood to be a body/soul composite, an intelligible union of meaningful motion, the substance of which constituted the living organism as a whole comprised of the basic principles of form and matter.

The human soul had its special properties, to be sure, which distinguished it from other animals (the powers of understanding and abstraction, for example) and this quality remains to this day the basis of the unsurpassable dignity of the human person among creatures. But teaching students about the immaterial/spiritual aspects of the human person in an exclusive way can run the risk of supposing that the only interest in developing a proper understanding of the human person is to defend immateriality. What can be lost in such a one-sided portrait are precisely the embodied dimensions of what it means to be a human being and all that goes with embodiment—including race, gender, class, and especially the vocation to steward the goods of the earth. In an attempt to defend a notion of the person against a reductive materialism, one also has to guard against an overemphasis on the spiritual aspects, thereby creating a kind of post-Cartesian angelism in Catholic guise.

The solution lies in promoting the conception of the human person as both spiritual *and* embodied, a substantial union of soul and body that was developed by St. Thomas and remains a vital philosophy of existence to this day.

This waning of a realist, earth-centered, creature-centered philosophical tradition would account, at least in part, both for the difficulty of Catholics to engage ecological issues in a distinctly Catholic manner today and the ever-increasing invisibility of the efforts to raise those concerns. It is not so much about the failure of the messengers as it is the increasing colorblindness concerning the theology of creation across the board.

Bright students could innocently wonder where the animals were raised and entire generations of Catholic farmers could grow up immune to the Church's theological vision of the dignity of their vocation as stewards of creation. The Holy Father could exhort us to consider creatures and their care and his message could be dismissed as a marginal curiosity—all due to the ever-evaporating confidence in creation and its relevance for understanding the human person within it. I am not so naïve as to think that things were better in earlier years, but I believe a good case can be made that things will get much worse in the future if we do not correct the systematic detachment of Catholic social and spiritual traditions from their essential ground: namely, this created earth upon which we live, move, and have our being.

What is needed for the new evangelization, in sum, is a new preparation for the ground upon which the reception of the Word might take root. We need to renew a philosophy of nature, of creation, for the next generation of Catholics. For it is only on the basis of reality that the Gospel of Christ can be built.

SELECTED READINGS FOR CHAPTER TWO

On an Agrarian Reading of the Bible

For an agrarian reading of the Bible, it is instructive that the sages treat agriculture as a primary realm in which God's wisdom is needed and utilized by humanity. Proverbs includes various instructions for farmers (e.g., 24:27;

27:23–27); moreover, the bad farmer is for the sages the epitome of . . . "sloth," the destructive quality that constitutes the antithesis of wisdom (24:30–34). . . . A wise farmer varies his work, observing the different moments of the agricultural task. These lines may also imply that the farmer matches his actions to the particular features of his own land—a necessity for all good farming, and particularly in the highly diverse uplands of Canaan, which can be worked successfully on in patches and small lots. A concern for scale in all uses of technology, for choosing a scale small enough so that the work matches the place, is for contemporary agrarians one of the marks of wisdom. . . . If we can see God's wise foundational work shaping our world, then we are ready to dispense with the false distinction between "practical work" on the one hand and "spiritual work" or "religious service" on the other, and likewise with the separation between scientific knowledge and practical wisdom. All our mental and physical activity should be directed toward shaping human life and (inescapably) the earth we must manage in order to survive, in accordance with the divine wisdom manifested in natural systems.

—Ellen Davis, *Scripture, Culture, and Agriculture: An Agrarian Reading of the Bible* (New York: Cambridge University Press, 2009), 34

On Aquinas and Contemporary Questions

Since the beginning of the twentieth century, and probably following the encouragement that successive popes have given to Christian reflection through their attention to political, economic, and social questions, we have seen the renewed reading of Thomas' oeuvre with an aim toward finding in it, if not direct answers to new problems, at least the principles that allow us to put the questions in their true light and, eventually, to discover some elements of a solution. . . . Without attempting an apology that would be out of place here we might say that Thomas' conception of creation is wholly suited to providing theological support for addressing the ecological worries of our time.

—Jean-Pierre Torrell, O.P., *Saint Thomas Aquinas, Volume 2: Spiritual Master*, trans. Robert Royal (Washington, DC: The Catholic University of America Press, 2003), 240–241

On What Catholics Are Called to Do

Catholics are called to value the goodness of God's creation both intrinsically and instrumentally. Catholics are called to aesthetically appreciate the beauty of God's creation. Catholics are called to give reverence to the sacramental Earth and universe because they manifest God's presence and character. Catholics are called to respect the various ways in which the diverse constituents of Earth praise God according to their natures. Catholics are called to cooperate with other species and systems to sustain the integrity of our planet. Catholics are called to be companions with other species within the dynamic web of life. Catholics are called to use other constituents of Earth with restraint and gratitude to God. Catholics are called to live morally virtuous lives in relation to one another and to other species and systems now and in the future. Catholics are called to love God's creation, especially the Earth. Furthermore, Catholics are called to see themselves within an all-inclusive context of other species, ecosystems, Earth and the entirety of the universe as called forth to completion by God. Valuing, appreciating, revering, respecting, cooperating, acting companionably, using with constraint and gratitude to God, living virtuously, and loving creation are characteristics that Catholics can develop in themselves and nurture in others. That these characteristics are exemplified in the Catholic theological tradition warrants their serious consideration and celebration.

—Jame Schaeffer, *Theological Foundations for Environmental Ethics: Reconstructing Patristic & Medieval Concepts* (Washington, DC: Georgetown University Press, 2009), 7–8

On the Limits of Scientific Methods

It cannot be maintained that empirical science provides a complete explanation of life, the interplay of all creatures and the whole of reality. This would be to breach the limits imposed by its own methodology. If we reason only within the confines of the latter, little room would be left for aesthetic sensibility, poetry, or even reason's ability to grasp the ultimate meaning and purpose of things. I would add that "religious classics can prove meaningful in every age; they have an enduring power to open new horizons. . . . Is it reasonable and enlightened to dismiss certain writings simply because they arose in the context of religious belief?" It would be quite simplistic to think that ethical principles present themselves purely in the abstract, detached from any context. Nor does the fact that they may be couched in religious language detract from their value in public debate. The ethical principles capable of being apprehended by reason can always reappear in different guise and find expression in a variety of languages, including religious language.

—Pope Francis, *LS*, no. 199

SELECTED RESOURCES FOR CHAPTER TWO

Woodene Koenig-Bricker, *Ten Commandments on the Environment: Pope Benedict XVI Speaks Out for Creation and Justice* (Notre Dame, IN: Ave Maria Press, 2009).

Jame Schaeffer, *Theological Foundations for Environmental Ethics: Reconstructing Patristic & Medieval Concepts* (Washington, DC: Georgetown University Press, 2009).

David Bovée, *The Church & The Land: The National Catholic Rural Life Conference and American Society, 1923–2007* (Washington, DC: The Catholic University of America Press, 2010).

CHAPTER THREE

Discerning Natural Law

"To hold creatures cheap is to slight the divine power."[1]

An azure dome is stretched taut to the bursting point. A roseate hue hangs like incense over the nave of the earth. Vespers is about to begin. "God come to my assistance . . ." And as the choral procession begins, a thousand grey-cloaked sandhill cranes settle into their stalls within the grassy marsh, chanting their familiar praises of evensong.

Few occasions register as deeply as that evening in Crex Meadows almost two decades ago, when the seasonal flight of the sandhill cranes came to a crescendo in central Wisconsin one October evening. I suppose that it was not more splendid than any other evening on the earth, were I to be paying attention, but that night I was *paying attention* and received a thousandfold in return.

"This is the eternal law," it came to me. This is the eternal law of the divine wisdom writ large in this small

[1] I *SCG* III, q. 69, in Gilby, 151.

portion of the universe. And I, a privileged creature in this splendid cosmos, am drawn just like them to participate in a manner unique to my own way of being. I, too, a "priest of this poor sacrifice," as Coleridge puts it,[2] offer my one life in praise, my prayer in the temple of creation.

Anyone who has had a glimpse of the beauty of the order of nature knows what I am talking about. In my nearly thirty years of teaching, no one has ever failed to recall an encounter with the beauty of the natural order. A certain amount of self-awareness and moral maturity is needed, I suppose, but the experience of awe is confirmed by all. Each one of us has had a moment of awe before the beauty of creation, before the goodness of things, the oneness of things, my connectedness among things, the peace of things. Try to capture it in words and you join the frustrated ranks of the ageless poets, philosophers, and theologians. Say a word aloud and the spell is broken, as silence seems to be a prerequisite. Take a selfie and you are altogether disqualified.

The point here is that the experience of beauty before the natural world is an interior moment. It may be common, but it is not to be shared. Stand on the precipice of Rainbow Curve in Rocky Mountain National Park, in tow with fellow citizens from virtually every corner on the earth, and the babble is reduced to silence. Hushed tones prevail. There is a natural reverence at work as contemplation replaces the banter.

The Thomist philosopher Josef Pieper, in the second

---

[2] Samuel Taylor Coleridge, "To Nature," in Samuel Taylor Coleridge, *The Complete Poems*, ed. William Keach (London: Penguin Classics, 1997).

half of his famous essay, *Leisure: The Basis of Culture*, speaks of the difference in meaning when we speak of something in a "location," something in an "environment," and something in a "world."[3]

What differentiates the proper usage, Pieper argues, is not a consideration of the object's ambient circumstances, but rather the distinct capacities of the object itself. Thus, we can speak of the location of a rock, the location of shale, or the location of oil, because rocks, shale, and oil are rather simple in their operations, their activities. When it comes to plants and animals, however, we can speak not only of their location, but now it is appropriate to speak of their environment, because plants and animals do not merely occupy a position; rather, they inhabit a place and they interact with the elements around them, drawing the immediate resources into their more complex operations.

But there is only one kind of creature, Pieper suggests, who occupies a world, a cosmos, and it is precisely the human person. The human person, with his or her capacity for intellectual comprehension and understanding, not only occupies a location, not only interacts with an environment, but is capable of unifying in a single intellectual insight the orbit of a world, a cosmos in which he or she is situated. And it is this unique spiritual capacity which renders all conversations about "humans and their environment" simply inadequate.

This is the unique spiritual capacity of the human person; it is what differentiates us from the rest of the created

---

[3] Josef Pieper, *Leisure: The Basis of Culture*, trans. Gerald Marlsbary (South Bend, IN: St. Augustine's Press, 1998), 98.

order; it is what establishes the basis of our claim to be the *imago Dei*; and it is what grounds our position in a world— as more than creatures inhabiting an environment. To be a human being, Pieper writes, "is to know things beyond the 'roof' of the stars, to go beyond the trusted enclosures of the normal . . . to go beyond the 'environment' to the 'world' in which that environment is enclosed."[4]

Thus, to persistently speak of humans and their environment without any reference to our status as intellectual creatures within an ordered cosmos is to reduce the human person to a mere animal among creatures. It is to deny the spiritual capacity of the human person as that intellectual being capable of unifying in a single intellectual apprehension, an ordered whole, a unified world.

Ironically, it was Sigurd Olson, a leading light among Minnesota naturalists, who first put me on to the insight of Josef Pieper, the Thomist. Olson alludes to Pieper's analysis to explain the phenomenon of "awe" he experienced as a guide and adventurer in the pristine lakes of the Boundary Waters Canoe Area Wilderness that runs along the northern Minnesota border with Canada.[5]

Olson takes a distinctly modern turn, however, and suggests that such moments of awe—moments in which we discern an order to the whole of experience—are due to the biological origins of our species. In Olson's view, the feeling of awe before the splendor of some wilderness space is the tug of the collective, biologically driven

---

4 Ibid., 94.
5 Sigurd F. Olson, "The Spiritual Need," in *The Meaning of Wilderness: Essential Articles and Speeches*, ed. David Backes (Minneapolis, MN: University of Minnesota Press, 2001), 139.

unconscious, the remnants of a past now long forgotten through the centuries of evolution and progress. Awe, for Olson, is an experience of tapping a repressed, collective memory.

Green Thomists propose a different phenomenology of awe before nature and suggest that the experience is not a mere harkening back toward some distant origin long past; rather, the experience of awe before the beauty of the created order is a glimpse into our ontological, not biological, origins. It is an intuition into our status as creatures within a cosmos, created by a God who is love. Awe is a glimpse of the gift of being.

Awe is, moreover, a privileged insight into our relationship with God and creation prior to the phenomenon of the Fall. Just as couples in their chaste, married love capture a glimpse of the prelapsarian state of innocence among the sexes as John Paul II has suggested in the development of his theology of the body, so too, the experience of awe, that kind of *ecstasis* encountered through the beauty of the created order and its goodness that so often accompanies an encounter with nature, can be understood as an intuition of that pre-fallen condition in which the alienation between the human person and creation did not exist.[6] In fact, Green Thomism stands in continuity with the theology of the body by proposing a "theology of embodiment," a fuller consideration of the body as the

---

[6] "Uniting with each other (in the conjugal act) so closely as to become 'one flesh,' man and woman, rediscover, so to speak, every time and in a special way, the mystery of creation." John Paul II, General Audience, November 21, 1979, in *The Theology of the Body: Human Love in the Divine Plan* (Boston: Daughters of Saint Paul, 1997), 49.

principle means by which the gift of being is received in every mode proper to the human person. As Thomas Dubay says, "The full experience of a rose requires that we see with our minds the inner energy, the hidden origin, the radical form, and not simply the manifested colors, shapes, and proportions." He continues, "Because our living intellects are rooted in our bodily/spiritual beings, we are attuned to the universe and can appreciate it as no mere animal can. . . . Only an intellect rooted in spirit can perceive and be thrilled by astronomy, microbiology, mathematics."[7]

For this reason alone, the Church should not be indifferent to preserving that encounter with the gift of creation today. For so many men and women in so many different ways, discovering the beauty of the natural order—whether in national parks or in more local venues—is that first tutor in the faith. It is that place where a presentiment of God, the reality of a divine presence, first invites itself into one's experience and imagination. As Pieper suggests, "the first wonder one feels forms the first step on the path that leads to the beatific vision, the state of blessedness resulting from reaching the Ultimate Cause. But that human nature is designed for nothing less than such an end, is proved by the ability of the human being to experience the wonder of creation."[8]

We might begin to appreciate the value of a wildlife "sanctuary," not merely as that space which protects a val-

---

[7] Thomas Dubay, S.M., *The Evidential Power of Beauty: Science and Theology Meet* (San Francisco: Ignatius Press, 1999), 65.
[8] Pieper, 104.

ued species and its habitat, but precisely as that space in which the human person, as a creature whom God has willed for divine communion, might begin an apprenticeship in his or her sacred vocation. By intentionally beholding the goodness of creation, we begin to share in the life of God and take the first steps in divine friendship. By entering into the receptive contemplation of created beauty, we shift from the more typical understanding of dominion over creation as a divinely sanctioned imperative to do something, and enter into the prior and deeper activity of simply beholding something. "Don't just do something! Stand there!" Green Thomism directs, for dominion over creation, so often understood as a mere *techne*, or mastery over creation, is properly manifest in imitating the divine posture before creation: the receptive contemplation of the goodness of things—indeed the very goodness of things.

We ought to be concerned to preserve the experience of the wilderness as a privileged occasion of divine theophany and understand the obligation we have to protect such spaces as precisely rooted in a larger vision of life as more than species inhabiting an environment, but as beloved children of Christ the Logos of the Creator, Christ the Logos of creation.

The Church's apparent silence on issues of the environment, then, is not because of the lack of concern for stewardship, a lack of appreciation for the integrity of creatures and the like. Rather the absence of any particular doctrinal tradition on environmental concerns as such emerges from the Church's steadfast refusal to understand the human person as a mere creature inhabiting an environment. We occupy a place in an ordered cosmos, a universal plan of redemption, "a common home," as Francis says, not merely an environment. Awe before the majesty of creation is less an experience of the environment, then, and more of an invitation to ponder the existential dimension of one's place in the universe—drawn from the abyss of nothing into the light of being and communion. Attending to the beauty of nature is to attend the inaugural lecture on self-knowledge.

This affirmation that there is an intelligence at work in the mystery of nature—that there is a wisdom to be discovered in the created order—lies at the heart of so many who champion an environmental sensitivity. It is only fitting to recognize that the same insight lies in the heart of the Church's vision as well. For what does it mean to "raise environmental awareness" if not the effort to more fully comprehend our place within the intelligible order of creation and our responsibility to live appropriately?

Yet, to conceive of such stewardship as an ever-deepening understanding of our participation in the eternal law does not further remove us from the theological tradition. In truth, it places us directly in its center, for to consider what it means to participate in the order of creation is precisely the definition of the natural law as promulgated through centuries of moral tradition. Natural law, Aquinas argues, is nothing more than the human being's participation in the eternal law of creation.[9] We can begin to see that developing an awareness of our responsibilities as creatures within a created order, as stewards of

9 *ST* I-II 91.2.

the environment as contemporary nomenclature puts it, is simply the extension of the natural law ethic into all areas of reasoned, embodied living.

There is a kind of affinity of outlook, in other words, between a stewardship that recognizes the value and integrity of creatures and their habitats and an outlook which affirms that there is divine wisdom at work in ordering the relationships among them. An appropriate understanding of stewardship would entail a deeper reflection upon how we are to participate within this divinely governed, divinely arranged wisdom. The issue of environmental stewardship simply raises the question: how should we participate within the eternal law that is manifest in the created order that surrounds us?

And yet to ponder how we ought to participate in the eternal law is simply to exercise one's conscience in light of natural law, that fundamental ordering of morality that governs our relationship to creation—now understood in an expanded sense— including not merely other creatures, but ourselves (and God) as well.

The tradition of natural law, so ably defended for centuries by Roman Catholic theologians and philosophers, supplies insights into how environmental stewardship ought to be properly conducted. For the natural law tradition would affirm not only the dignity and value of the various creatures and our relationship to them, but it would begin to outline more completely how human beings are to treat the environment within the context of their just relationships to one another.

More to the point, recasting environmental stewardship as the fundamental expression of natural law would also serve to retain all of the critical moral insights concerning the dignity of the human person and place them within the overall approach to the question. By drawing ecology into the umbrella of natural law, the perennial tensions between environmental and pro-life movements could begin to be dismantled. For the task of the Catholic intellectual—theologians, philosophers, and environmentalists—would be to articulate more fully how the natural law extends to a consideration of not just human beings in some isolated abstraction, but as fully enfleshed participants in the material order itself.

Natural law has fallen on hard times in many intellectual circles, but its traditional defenders might begin to see in the widespread emergence of environmental sensitivity the light of conscience, the rebellion of a culture deprived of the normativity of nature by an intellectual habit of mind which places *techne,* or technical skill, over *sapientia,* or wisdom. Renewing confidence in the wisdom of creation and the moral obligations to live reasonably in accord with it will serve to support a notion of stewardship and reinvigorate the moral tradition.

That evening in Crex Meadows was an inaugural primer in the natural law of human flourishing. My participation in the eternal law was no longer that of a bloodless, rational agent conjuring ends and dispatching purposes for some lower ranks of animal flesh to enact. I was one man, a substantial union of body and spirit, a creature within this magnificent cosmos of created natures, under the gaze of God.

That is the rhythm of human flourishing on earth; that is the natural law of our being in the world. The gift of things comes first, receptive contemplation comes next—and then God dawns before all. Natural law is that way of being-in-the-world proper to humans. The human soul, wedded to this glorious earth through the communion of its body, lives out a manner of flourishing exclusive to a rational animal. If there is a privilege to our status, it is that of servant leaders who draw into the recesses of consciousness, that "light by which we see light," in order that we might serve creation and honor the Creator by living a life of humility and praise. In the company of the world, the human soul drinks light and pours forth praise. *Magnificat anima mea Dominum, et exultavit . . . !* (Lk 1:46–47).

SELECTED READINGS FOR CHAPTER THREE

On the Nature of Moral Obligation

All obligation is based upon being. Reality is the foundation of ethics. The good is that which is in accord with reality. He who wishes to know and to do the good must turn his gaze upon the objective world of being. Not upon his own "ideas," not upon his "conscience," not upon "values," not upon arbitrarily established "ideals and "models." He must turn away from his own act and fix his eyes upon reality. . . . to be good means to be directed toward realization. . . . But to be directed toward realization means also to be directed in accordance with the inherent direction of the potentiality of all things: it means an affirmation of all created being, "love" for all that is; it means desiring for and granting to every being its peculiar form of realization. All this must be thought of as completely free from any philanthropic self-complacent sentimentality. . . . Reality is the basis of the good. This means for our present purpose, according to the meaning of "real"—*realis*, that to be good is to do justice to objective being; that is good which corresponds to "the thing"; the good is that which is in accord with objective reality.

—Josef Pieper, "Reality and the Good" in *Living the Truth* (San Francisco, CA: Ignatius Press, 1989), 111–112

On Whether Corporeal Creatures Are from God

I answer that, certain heretics maintain that visible things are not created by the good God, but by an evil principle, and allege in proof of their error the words of the Apostle (2 Cor. 4.4) "The god of this world hath blinded the minds of unbelievers." But this position is altogether untenable. . . . Corporeal creatures according to their nature are good, though this good is not universal, but partial and limited, the consequence of which is a certain opposition of contrary qualities, though each quality is good in itself. To those, however, who estimate things, not by the nature thereof, but by the good they themselves can derive therefrom, everything which is harmful to themselves seems simply evil. For they do not reflect that what is in some way injurious to one person, to another is beneficial, and that even to themselves the same thing may be evil in some respects, but good in others.

—St. Thomas Aquinas, *ST* I 65.1; I 65.1 ad 2

On Creation as Teaching Us of God

God has written a precious book, "whose letters are the multitude of created things present in the universe." The Canadian bishops rightly pointed out that no creature is excluded from this manifestation of God: "From panoramic vistas to the tiniest living form, nature is a constant source of wonder and awe. It is also a continuing revelation of the divine." The bishops of Japan, for their part, made a thought-provoking observation: "To sense each creature singing the hymn of its existence is to live joyfully in God's love and hope." This contemplation of creation allows us to discover in each thing a teaching which God wishes to hand on to us, since "for the believer, to contemplate creation is to hear a message, to listen to a paradoxical and silent voice." We can say that "alongside revelation properly so-called, contained in sacred Scripture, there is a divine manifestation in the blaze of the sun and the fall of night." Paying attention to this manifestation, we learn to see ourselves in relation to all other creatures: "I express myself in expressing the world; in my effort to decipher the sacredness of the world, I explore my own."

—Pope Francis, *LS*, no. 85

On the Variety within Creation

The universe as a whole, in all its manifold relationships, shows forth the inexhaustible riches of God. Saint Thomas Aquinas wisely noted that multiplicity and variety "come from the intention of the first agent," who willed that "what was wanting to one in the representation of the divine goodness might be supplied by another," inasmuch as God's goodness "could not be represented fittingly by any one creature." Hence we need to grasp the variety of things in their multiple relationships. We understand better the importance and meaning of each creature if we contemplate it within the entirety of God's plan.

—Pope Francis, *LS*, no. 86

SELECTED RESOURCES FOR CHAPTER THREE

Pierre-Marie Emonet, O.P., *The Dearest Freshness Deep Down Things: An Introduction to the Philosophy of Being*, trans. Robert R. Barr (New York: The Crossroad Publishing Company, 1999).

Jean Mouroux, *The Meaning of Man*, trans. A. H. G. Downes (New York: Image Books, 1961).

Wendell Berry, *Life is a Miracle: An Essay Against Modern Superstition* (Washington, DC: Counterpoint, 2000).

CHAPTER FOUR

The Gift of *Laudato si'*

"Nothing but his goodness moves God to produce things."[1]

It is especially in this light of the natural law that *Laudato si'* emerges as an extraordinary encyclical.[2] Through it the Holy Father reaffirms the central thesis of the natural law tradition: that because everything is created by a loving Father, we inhabit an earth which we share with His creatures. Thus the gift of this beautiful earth is not to be ignored nor regretted; this world is, rather, the central setting in which the Christian life is to be attentively lived and joyfully pursued. Life is not a dress rehearsal for the Christian. This *is* the Christian life—partial, hopeful, expectant, promissory, yet to be fulfilled—but no less real than that of beatitude. Here, on this patch of soil, I either love the Lord and keep His earth or I don't.

---

[1] *SCG* II, 46, in Gilby, 157.

[2] Portions of this chapter are taken from my essay, "The Treasure of *Laudato Si*'" in *Principles: A Publication of Christendom College* 1, no. 3 (2015): 1–7.

The putative subject matter of *Laudato si'* is the ecological concerns that have emerged at the conclusion of the twentieth century as a result of the practical abuses consonant with industrialization and modern development. But *Laudato si'* is much more than a meditation taking aim at modern environmental practices and policies. It is a magisterial call to recover creation itself, and in recovering creation discover the moral fabric that binds us to ourselves, each other, each creature, and the Creator. Indeed, there is scarcely an aspect of contemporary life that is not addressed in some fashion in the encyclical. Its breadth, however, does not suggest anything trivial. Instead, it affirms the foundational character of the discussion the Holy Father seeks to undertake.

Taken as a set of practical observations in isolation from the broader theological implications, *Laudato si'* does not constitute an extraordinary moment. It merely reiterates some of the conclusions and findings of both the scientific and ethical communities. And yet, when read against the broader claims of theological reasoning, *Laudato si'* marks the occasion of historic theological development.

Simply stated, *Laudato si'* calls for an "integral ecology" that advances a comprehensive vision of our place as beloved creatures of a cosmos.[3] It is a mandate to retrieve the natural law in the twenty-first century and beyond. Not the rarified, conceptualist accounts one sometimes encounters in the scholarship of the postmodern milieu, but the fully enfleshed, perennial articulation which sees the spontaneous inclinations of human aspirations with-

---

[3] *LS,* no. 137

in a broader movement of a universal attraction to God expressed in the drama of every creature's living, where God is both inspiration and end.[4] Each creature, Thomas affirms, bears the impress of the divine and seeks, however feeble its powers, to manifest His glory to the best of its ability. *Laudato si'* affirms as much; it is a manifesto for Green Thomism.[5]

The Holy Father's claim that "everything is connected" is not a mere sentimental, nostalgic, or poetic fancy; his aim is to affirm a doctrinal claim: "Nature is nothing other than a certain kind of art, namely God's art, impressed upon things, whereby those things are moved to a determinate end."[6] For God is the Creator of all things and thus, "each creature has its own purpose." Moreover, "the entire material universe speaks of God's love. . . . the universe as a whole, in all its manifold relationships, shows forth the inexhaustible riches of God."[7]

Laudato si' consistently relies upon a theology of "nature" as divinely arranged, an ordered complex of organic wholes each with its own note of intelligence, together

---

[4] For an excellent account of various approaches to the meaning and significance of "nature" in natural law ethics, see Matthew Levering, *Biblical Natural Law: A Theocentric and Teleological Approach* (New York: Oxford University Press, 2008).

[5] For an account of the importance of Thomism for developing an integral ecology, see the collection of essays derived from a 2009 symposium hosted by The Saint Paul Seminary School of Divinity entitled "Renewing the Face of the Earth: The Church and the Order of Creation," in *Nova et Vetera* 10, no. 1 (2012): 61–278; especially, "Perennial Wisdom: Notes Toward a Green Thomism," 67–80.

[6] *LS*, no. 80, citing Thomas Aquinas, *In octo libros Physicorum Aristotelis expositio*, Lib. II, lectio 14.

[7] *LS*, nos. 84, 86

forming a symphony of meaning in motion—a theology of nature which has been honed over the centuries through the Church's repeated engagement with its central questions. Whether in its encounter with the Manicheans of the fourth century, the Albigensians of the thirteenth, or the Materialists of the twenty-first, the Church's consistent witness has been on behalf of the order, beauty, and goodness of creation. Francis' encyclopedic appeal to witnesses from the ancient tradition (as well as more recent bishops' statements from around the globe) demonstrates that *Laudato si'* is the magisterial expression of that core conviction in the twenty-first century. Its central significance lies in the clear affirmation that the native habitat of the human person, as a spiritual creature, is precisely this material cosmos of organic beings. The human person, whose dignity lies within a spiritual destiny, is nevertheless a creature of this beautiful earth—a living, organic being among other organic beings whose immortal soul by nature transcends the cosmos and yet by grace permeates it with eternal significance.

In this sense *Laudato si'* poses a fundamental question to every citizen of the globe: How do you and I, as human beings, as sons and daughters of the Father, flourish within this divinely ordered cosmos? As such, one can read the document as an extended meditation upon and application of the natural law, for natural law is nothing other than those principles of moral discernment that emerge from the affirmation that we are rational creatures participating in a divinely ordered reality, otherwise known as the eternal law.[8] Francis' aim is to make relevant to twenty-first century audiences the moral imperatives that follow the natural inclinations all of us pursue as creatures drawn to flourishing by the call of a loving Father.

That the phrase "natural law" itself is absent from the document is not determinative, for the nomenclature surrounding natural law ethics in the modern academy has increasingly been cast as an ethic set within a cosmos devoid of a natural teleology.[9] Francis himself alludes to the shifting valuation of "nature" in contemporary culture.[10] Nonetheless, natural law provides the theological warrant for *Laudato si'* because as the International Theological Commission had already stated in 2009, "There cannot be an adequate response to the complex questions of ecology except within the framework of a deeper understanding of the natural law, which places value on the connection between the human person, society, culture, and the equilibrium of the bio-physical sphere in which the human person is incarnate."[11]

Or as the Dominican scholar Mieczysław A. Krąpiec, O.P., tells it, "[The] affirmation or a transgression of the Eternal Divine Law does not take place in an abstraction nor directly in relation to God Himself. Rather, it

---

[8] *ST* I-II 91. 2.

[9] Steven A. Long, *Natura Pura: On the Recovery of Nature in the Doctrine of Grace* (New York: Fordham University Press, 2010).

[10] *LS*, no. 78

[11] International Theological Commission, *In Search of a Universal Ethic: A New Look at the Natural Law* (2009), 82. Hereafter, ITC. For a similar perspective on related matters, see William C. French, "Natural Law and Ecological Responsibility: Drawing on the Thomistic Tradition," *University of St. Thomas Law Journal* 5, no. 1 (2008): 12–39.

takes place through the composition of things . . . with which we either do or do not reckon in our conduct."[12] In other words, to live out the principles of the natural law requires more than meeting some epistemic condition of internal coherence within one's own self-directing principles; rather, precisely because of the kind of creatures we are (embodied, organic beings inhabiting a cosmos), enactment of natural law is inescapably yoked to prior relationships with the given order of creatures. Francis weaves this moral and organic character of the natural law into a singular insight of a participated ethics. He says,

> Neglecting to monitor the harm done to nature and the environmental impact of our decisions is only the most striking sign of a disregard for the message contained in the structures of nature itself. When we fail to acknowledge as part of reality the worth of a poor person, a human embryo, a person with disabilities—to offer just a few examples—it becomes difficult to hear the cry of nature itself; everything is connected. Once the human being declares independence from reality and behaves with absolute dominion, the very foundations of our life begin to crumble. . .[13]

Notwithstanding the rational character of our participation in the eternal law, we do so in a distinctly human

---

[12] Mieczysław A. Krąpiec, O.P., *I—Man: An Outline of Philosophical Anthropology*, trans. Marie Lescoe, Andrew Woznicki, and Theresa Sandok, et. al. (New Britain, CT: Mariel Publications, 1983), 229–230.
[13] *LS*, no. 117.

manner, namely, as embodied creatures of the earth. And thus our participation, our inclinations, are inescapably woven within the fabric of relations that makes our living human. The natural law, at its core, asks the question: how do I as a rational animal among animals reasonably flourish within this theonomically-ordered cosmos?

Laudato si' permanently disowns Cartesian nostalgia and (thankfully) delivers the final eulogy on modernity. "An inadequate presentation of Christian anthropology," Francis says, "gave rise to a wrong understanding of the relationship between human beings and the world."[14] He demands, instead, that we recover the analysis of human flourishing which includes the participation of other embodied creatures within the divinely arranged cosmos. The specific difference, the *rationis*, can no longer eclipse the genus, *animalia*; the *cogito* can no longer silence the *habito*. "Often, what was handed on was a Promethean vision of mastery over the world, which gave the impression that the protection of nature was something that only the faint-hearted cared about. Instead, our 'dominion' over the universe should be understood more properly in the sense of responsible stewardship."[15]

What is integral ecology? It is the intentional practice of those principles of human flourishing that emerge from the reasoned pursuit of a hierarchy of goods to which we are spontaneously inclined, a pursuit that we enact alongside every other creature of the universe, a pursuit that is happily ordered toward goods that are perfective of us

---

[14] *LS*, no. 116.
[15] Ibid.

as creatures within a common home. Integral ecology is forward thinking as it considers the prudential use of the goods of the earth. It is justice oriented as it considers what is owed to neighbors in good faith and community. It is temperate in seeking the least reckless, most conservative use of resources. It is courageous in its vision of community, which includes those most often marginalized as well as the environments in which they live.

These natural virtues of integral ecology, imbued with a living presence of Christ, are infused with a zeal for Him to be known and loved—not only as Lord, but as Logos. In Christ, prudence becomes proactive and not merely strategic; generosity replaces efficiency. It puts the needs of others (those present and those imagined as future citizens) in higher priority than mere economics might demand. Justice calls us to outcompete one another in love and consider the richest sense of what is due to others beyond even their own imagining. Temperance deliberately seeks the *more* modest means, not merely the well-balanced or measured pace. And courage lives in joyful hope for the eschatological renewal of the entire order of creation. This universal attraction of the love of God, Pope Francis affirms, "is the basis of our conviction that, as part of the universe, called into being by one Father, all of us are linked by unseen bonds and together form a kind of universal family, a sublime communion which fills us with a sacred, affectionate and humble respect."[16]

In *Laudato si'* Francis does more than simply reiterate a vision of natural law. The single greatest achievement

---

[16] *LS*, no. 89.

lies in his effort to develop it: extensively and intensively. Extensively, he expands the circle of ethical concern to include a rational evaluation of those creatures of the environment that share in the universal call to wholeness. In much the same way Aldo Leopold attempted nearly fifty years ago in his *A Sand County Almanac*, Francis demands that we now include the biotic community in a vision of bioethical considerations. Intensively, Francis focuses moral evaluation on the embodied character of natural human flourishing. Habituated as we are to speaking of human dignity in terms of the immortal soul, or liberty, or autonomy, or rationality, or personhood, we can sometimes forget the other half of the equation: that the human soul belongs to a human body. There is no "I" that is not "me."[17] I am someone who is inescapably somewhere. There is always a "place" in the landscape of humanity, a location, an environment in which ensouled soil, soiled souls, seek perfection. Whether we till the soil directly or live off the labor of those who do, each one—everyone—reveals the dust from whence we came. To till it and to keep it is thus part of the pledge to God and each other.

In sum, "There can be no ecology without an adequate anthropology."[18] One might add, "and vice versa." For the very conditions that constitute an adequate anthropology include a consideration of the ecological conditions in which the "anthropos" flourishes. It is not irrelevant to my argument that the International Theological Commission, precisely in its efforts to provide a robust account of

[17] *ST* I 75 4.
[18] *LS*, no. 118.

the importance of the natural law, captures the essential thrust of *Laudato si'* when it states:

> An integral ecology must promote what is specifically human, all the while valuing the world of nature in its physical and biological integrity. In fact, even if man, as a moral being who searches for the ultimate truth and the ultimate good, transcends his own immediate environment, he does so by accepting the special mission of keeping watch over the natural world, living in harmony with it, and defending vital values without which neither human life nor the biosphere of this planet can be maintained. This integral ecology summons every human being and every community to a new responsibility. It is inseparable from a global political orientation respectful of the requirements of the natural law.[19]

What for centuries has been devolving into an option for Christian living (and in many instances ignored entirely) has now been declared an essential facet of the Christian way. Creatures matter because their Creator matters; to confess Christ is to care for the creatures He enlivens. By retrieving *natura*, that is, creation in its splendor, from the brink of ethical oblivion, "integral ecology" has officially been declared a fitting species of moral theology. No longer the muse of transcendentalist whimsy (something supposedly only the fainthearted cared about), nor the

---

[19] ITC, 82. Note the use of "integral ecology."

blunt instrument of bourgeois bureaucrats, ecology—the *scientia* of our common home—has been redeemed and declared "integral" by the gospel of creation.

Some may think it sufficient to simply affirm the union of the body/soul composite as the shibboleth of Catholic anthropology. It is not. For while it may be true that the human soul is apt for the body, St. Thomas repeatedly insists that the composite is apt for the universe, that phantasmagoria of intelligible objects, any one of which is the proper delight of human understanding. The body is for the sake of the soul—true enough. But the soul's powers are made fecund not on account of the body alone, but by the presence of the objects which enliven it.

The soul knows by means of knowable objects. It is on account of the presence of these sensible objects that we live in a world that makes sense. Disembodied souls may flourish in a vat of some miraculous liquor; Green Thomists cannot.[20] Their native habitat is the glorious cosmos of intelligible objects whose existence is freely scattered by God in all manner of flora and fauna. Each creature bears the *vestigia Dei*, the impress of God, indeed the *vestigia Trinitate*, the impress of the Trinity.[21] Creatures can lead us to God,[22] and precisely through their witness to hope they give evidence of the divine intellect at work

---

[20] "Descartes was asking for absolute certainty from a brain-in-a-vat, a certainty that was not needed when the brain (or the mind) was firmly attached to its body and the body thoroughly involved in its normal ecology." Bruno Latour, *Pandora's Hope: Essays on the Reality of Science Studies* (Cambridge, MA: Harvard University Press, 1999), 4.

[21] See *ST* I 45.7; *LS*, no. 239.

[22] See *ST* I 65.1 ad 3.

among us.[23] Taken as a whole they manifest the divine goodness even more perfectly than when considered in isolation.[24] Such themes permeate St. Thomas' work and run throughout the text of *Laudato si'*.

The stakes could not be higher in terms of a charter for renewing Christendom. In this age of technocratic *eros*, the new evangelization of culture will come to nothing if it does not include the unequivocal affirmation of the splendor of things upon which authentic Christian culture depends. Culture marks the intersection of the material and the spiritual realms. Neither angels nor antelope inhabit one. Lacking the requisite need for the body, the angelic world has no use of a culture in which it may know itself, through which it may express itself. The body, and all that goes with embodiment, is alien to the world of angels: place, location, region, and locale. There is no "local food movement" concerning the communion of the angels, as there is nothing particularly local to their natures. This is not to argue that the beatitude of the angels is somehow imperfect because it lacks the qualities of the brutes—a position Thomas describes precisely as *omnino absurdum*—completely absurd.[25] But it is to argue that we ought not aspire to angelic beatitude. The task of culture is a vocation properly given to the embodied creature and ought to be celebrated as a feature of our particular excellence. As C. S. Lewis puts it, speaking of angels and us:

---

[23] See *ST* I-II 40.3.
[24] *ST* I 47.1; *LS*, no. 86.
[25] *SCG* IV 83.13.

They see the Form of Air; but mortals breathing it
Drink the whole summer down into the breast.

The lavish pinks, the field new-mown, the ravishing
Sea-smells, the wood-fire smoke that whispers Rest.

The tremor on the rippled pool of memory
That from each smell in widening circles goes,
The pleasure and the pang—can angels measure it?
An angel has no nose.[26]

Ours is soulful soil and all that accompanies ensoilment: place, region, locale, terroir, history and heritage, aroma and timbre, tint and texture, and race, and gender, and class. Our knowledge and love is clotted with the clay of earthiness, bound to the muck and matter of things. This is the marvelous medium through which Christ is known and loved! The fabric of Christian culture is made glorious through the warp and woof of human labor, spirit, and intelligence. The craftsman becomes an agent of evangelization, permeating matter with spirit and intelligence. Through the most intimate exchange of the body with things—through touch and taste, smell and sight, the artist gives birth to the interior word of both the medium and the master for the sake of the world.

Culture is the privilege given to those who pursue excellence through the splendor of stuff. It is marvelous when we seize the opportunity to give voice to our com-

---

[26] C. S. Lewis, "On Being Human," in C. S. Lewis, *Poems*, ed. Walter Hooper (San Diego, CA: Harcourt, Inc., 1992), 34.

mon dignity through its venues of art and music, dance and craft. It is a sorry state of affairs when it slackens to the level of mere brutishness or becomes the plaything of disaffected elites. Neither an instinct nor an abstraction, culture is the vocation of embodied, rational beings at play in the universe of things.

Culture, moreover, is not simply the effect of spirit on matter; but matter, too, shapes the spirit—a dialectic of region and reason unfolds. Place gives rise to style and vice versa.

"If I should die, think only this of me," Rupert Brooke implores, "that there's some corner of a foreign field / That is for ever England."[27] For certain, Brooke's reflections about a soldier in World War I seem a long way from immediate concerns. And yet the poem has always evoked in me a theme that dominates my imagination when it comes to culture: the human person is of the earth, and it is because we are embodied that we can claim such affinity with the soil beneath us.

Continuing with Brooke, if he were to die and be buried elsewhere than England:

> ... There shall be
>   In that rich earth a richer dust concealed;
> A dust whom England bore, shaped, made aware,
>   Gave, once, her flowers to love, her ways to roam,
> A body of England's, breathing English air,
>   Washed by the rivers, blest by suns of home.[28]

---

[27] Rupert Brooke, "The Soldier," in *Collected Poems* (Cambridge, MA: Oleander Press, 2010), 139.

[28] Ibid.

The "richer dust concealed" here is Brooke's own body, a body shaped and made by English culture. His body, like every human body, is marked with the sign of the place, the region, from which the body is formed. We're so used to speaking of human dignity in terms of an immortal soul that we can sometimes forget our place. We can forget that the human soul belongs to a human body, a body that comes from the soil, a body that dwells in a culture.

The culture of a rural life, for example, is a constant witness to this bond with the earth. Its rhythms are kept by the seasons and their temperaments. Fall's frenetic pace gives way to winter's quiet. Spring gets poised for a comeback—though not for a while. The farmer partners with the earth in hopes of a yield, a cooperative is formed and the fruits are coaxed from the silent strength that is nature. Bent with the shape of labor, the farmer bears in his body the signs of his husbandry. The earth shapes him as he shapes the earth.

But each of us is like the farmer, yoked to the soil, because each of us, as a human, is a creature of soil. All of us share in this heritage, the earth. And so all of us are bound to the soil in some manner or other. We know by faith that our destiny lies beyond; but our legacy begins here, from the earth, of the earth. And care for the earth and its resources is an extension of care for one another, as creatures drawn from the soil and returned to it . . . for a time, anyway.

It was World War I that provided the occasion for Brooke to pen the immortal words of the poem "The Soldier." His "corner of a foreign field" was somewhere along the Dardanelles, a narrow strait just east of northwest Turkey, nearly half the globe away from Brooke's native

England. Brooke himself died en route and never surrendered his life in battle directly, but the theme is nonetheless pertinent: my body is a vestige of the earth and bears in its features the culture out of which my community is crafted. To commit to building a culture of life means committing ourselves to the care of the earth out of which every culture gets its name.

It bears repeating: Christianity is not a set of abstract prescriptions nurtured in the labyrinthine ways of one's own mind. It is not an amalgam of gnostic insights of a privileged few. Christianity makes the claim that the Logos ordinarily discerned in the splendor of being has extraordinarily become flesh in the person of Jesus Christ. "In the beginning was the Word, and the Word was with God and the Word was God. . . . all things were made through him, and without him was not anything made that was made. . . . we have beheld his glory . . ." (Jn 1:1, 3, 14).

Stir the embers and follow them on their way toward the stars, or ascend to the summit and rest amidst the clouds, welcome the roseate tips of dawn or rest in the light of a waxing moon—and grace will flood the soul with a pure gift of truth: all of this is not merely something to behold; it is a call from someone to behold, the Logos of God. The world takes its cue from a Who, not a what. I delight in the group message of the world writ large. It is addressed to me.

What every hill and glen confirm, every swell or ebb announce, every flashing cataract or placid pool declare, every fretted flight or unperturbed pace suggest, the text message goes out to all the world: "All is good, because I am good, and I love you."

The invisible source of all creation, one and the same Logos, is made visible in the person of Jesus Christ. Christ, the Logos made flesh, *is* the one through whom all things are made. No Catholic is indifferent to the surrounding world because we are not indifferent to the Word of whom it speaks.[29] For the love poetry of the earth is never dead; the Poet still speaks in things through the grammar of creation in the lexicon of love.[30]

Laudato si' draws from this aquifer of metaphysics-made-wine with the event of Christ and relies upon a natural theology which provides, among other things, a portrait of an ordered universe utterly dependent upon a provident God whose causality extends to the operations of individuals, every individual—their coherence, as well as their purpose. As Pope Francis puts it, "Our insistence that each human being is an image of God should not make us overlook the fact that each creature has its own purpose. None is superfluous. The entire material universe speaks of God's love, his boundless affection for us. Soil, water, mountains: everything is, as it were, a caress of God."[31]

Pope Francis' encyclical is an extraordinary achievement and has the capacity to inspire in the twenty-first century what the mendicants inspired in the thirteenth. That the appeal here is to St. Thomas and not so much to St. Francis as the hermeneutic of continuity in this chapter is not intended in any exclusive sense. It is merely to affirm what has transpired through the ages: the poet of

---

[29] *LS*, no. 83.
[30] See John Keats, "On the Grasshopper and the Cricket," in *John Keats: Complete Poems* (Harvard University Press, 2003), 54.
[31] *LS*, no. 84.

Laudato si' inspires us to action and the poet of *"Pange Lingua"* illumines the way. Whatever the legacy invoked, one can count on Green Thomists to sing as they go.

SELECTED READINGS FOR CHAPTER FOUR

On the Natural Law and the Natures of Things

The key insight is that all moral truth arises from the nature of things, true in themselves and in crucial respects accessible to reason. Every being has a nature, and that nature defines the ends and ultimate good for which it exists. In discerning these purposes we perceive what that being is, what it can do, what it must do to find its completion and fulfillment, and therefore what its moral interests are and how they may be advanced or hindered. Suddenly all is not arbitrary and we have a fixed point of reference, an intelligent basis for calling one thing good and another bad. That which advances a being toward its natural fulfillment is good. That which frustrates or perverts its natural development is bad. . . .

Antiquated though "natural law" may sound, it holds up. It provides the only rational grounds I know of for claiming any one thing better than another, without reliance on religious belief or intuition or the constructs of theory. . . . Modern philosophers tend to view the assumption of natural law as an archaic obstacle to enlightenment and progress because it obliges us to acknowledge some things as simply true whether we like it or not. But they have carried mankind a long way, the assumptions of natural law, and for that reason alone command our careful attention. Whether natural law accords with one's own bold new theories or not, it still happens to be the central moral principle underlying Western civil society, democracy and the rights and protections we all claim for ourselves. Natural law is more revolutionary than any scheme of rights ever conceived precisely because it does affirm an authority higher than ourselves and those who rule over us.

—Matthew Scully, *Dominion: The Power of Man, the Suffering of Animals, and the Call to Mercy* (New York: St. Martin's Press, 2002), 299–301

On Whether in Creatures Is Necessarily Found a Trace of the Trinity

Every effect in some degree represents its cause, but diversely. For some effects represent only the causality of the cause, but not its form; as smoke represents fire. Such a representation is called a "trace": for a trace shows that someone has passed by but not who it is. Other effects represent the cause as regards the similitude of its form, as fire generated represents fire generating; and a statue of Mercury represents Mercury; and this is called the representation of "image." Now the processions of the Divine Persons are referred to the acts of intellect and will, as was said above. For the Son proceeds as the word of the intellect; and the Holy Ghost proceeds as love of the will. Therefore, in rational creatures, possessing intellect and will, there is found the representation of the Trinity by way of image, inasmuch as there is found in them the word conceived, and the love proceeding.

But in all creatures there is found the trace of the Trinity inasmuch as in every creature are found some things which are necessarily reduced to the Divine Persons as to their cause. For every creature subsists in its own being, and has a form, whereby it is determined to a species, and has relation to something else. Therefore as it is a created substance, it represents the cause and principle; and so in that manner it shows the Person of the Father, Who is the "principle from no principle." According as it has a form and species, it represents the Word as the form of the thing made by art is from the conception of the craftsman. According as it has relation of order, it represents the Holy Ghost inasmuch as He is love, because the order of the effect to something else is from the will of the Creator. And therefore Augustine says [*De Trin.* vi 10] that the trace of the Trinity is found in every creature, according "as it is one individual," and according "as it is formed by a species," and according as it "has a certain relation of order." And to these also are reduced those three, "number," "weight," and "measure," mentioned in the Book of Wisdom (9:21). For "measure" refers to the substance of the thing limited by its principles, "number" refers to the species, "weight" refers to the order. And to these three are reduced the other three mentioned by Augustine [*De Nat. Boni* iii], "mode," "species," and "order," and also those he mentions [QQ. 83, qu. 18]: "that which exists; whereby it is distinguished; whereby it agrees." For a thing exists by its substance, is distinct by its form, and agrees by its order. . . .

—St. Thomas Aquinas, *ST* I 45.7

On the Nature of Ecological Conversion

This [ecological] conversion calls for a number of attitudes which together foster a spirit of generous care, full of tenderness. First, it entails gratitude and gratuitousness, a recognition that the world is God's loving gift, and that we are called quietly to imitate his generosity in self-sacrifice and good works: "Do not let your left hand know what your right hand is doing . . . and your Father who sees in secret will reward you" (Mt 6:3-4). It also entails a loving awareness that we are not disconnected from the rest of creatures, but joined in a splendid universal communion. As believers, we do not look at the world from without but from within, conscious of the bonds with which the Father has linked us to all beings. By developing our individual, God-given capacities, an ecological conversion can inspire us to greater creativity and enthusiasm in resolving the world's problems and in offering ourselves to God "as a living sacrifice, holy and acceptable" (Rom 12:1). We do not understand our superiority as a reason for personal glory or irresponsible dominion, but rather as a different capacity which, in its turn, entails a serious responsibility stemming from our faith.

—Pope Francis, *LS*, no. 220.

On Inconvenient Truths

In the words of Augustine, "If an unskilled person enters the workshop of an artificer he sees in it many appliances of which he does not understand the use, and which, if he is a foolish fellow, he considers unnecessary. Moreover, should he carelessly fall into the fire, or wound himself with a sharp-edged tool, he is under the impression that many of the things there are hurtful; whereas the craftsman, knowing their use, laughs at his folly. And thus some people presume to find fault with many things in this world through not seeing the reasons for their existence. For though not required for the furnishing of our house, these things are necessary for the perfection of the universe." And, since man before he sinned would have used the things of this world conformably to the order designed, poisonous animals would not have injured him.

—St. Thomas Aquinas *ST* I 72.1 ad 6

SELECTED RESOURCES FOR CHAPTER FOUR

Marie George, *Stewardship of Creation: What Catholics Should Know about Church Teaching on the Environment* (Indianapolis, IN: St. Catherine of Siena Press, 2009).

Matthew Scully, *Dominion: The Power of Man, the Suffering of Animals, and the Call to Mercy* (New York: St. Martin's Press, 2002).

Thomas Nagel, *Mind and Cosmos: Why the Materialist Neo-Darwinian Conception of Nature is Almost Certainly False* (Oxford, UK: Oxford University Press, 2012).

·✦·

CHAPTER FIVE

THE NATURE OF NATURE

"Homes are not beautiful if they are empty. Things are beautiful by the indwelling of God."[1]

2014 marked the fiftieth anniversary of the Wilderness Act. Signed into law by Lyndon B. Johnson, the act was the first piece of federal legislation to forever designate some nine million acres of land as "Wilderness Places," putting them under the protection of the newly created National Wilderness Preservation System. Today, that system includes more than 110 million acres, and for many people the passage of the Wilderness Act marks one of America's greatest achievements concerning the protection of our heritage and the promotion of the common good.

There is a simple text at its core: "A wilderness, in contrast with those areas where man and his own works dominate the landscape, is hereby recognized as an area where the earth and its community of life are untrammeled by man, where man himself is a visitor who does

---

[1] Aquinas, *Exposition on the Psalms* xxv, 5, in Gilby, 79.

not remain." The Act goes on to state that such land is to be understood to retain its "primeval character and influence," to have been "shaped primarily by the forces of nature," and to have outstanding opportunities for such things as "solitude."[2]

The language is succinct and poetic and stands in sharp contrast to the more plodding prose typical of government legislation. More importantly, the language points to underlying claims, implicit convictions about the meaning of nature, its place in our lives, the role and significance of nature in the development of character, and the common good of the country. Commenting on the importance of wilderness in our collective imagination, the advocate and novelist Wallace Stegner says that even if some of us are never able to enter wild spaces, we can still contemplate the idea of wilderness. "Take pleasure in the fact that such a timeless and uncontrolled part of earth is still there. For it can be a means," he says, "of reassuring ourselves of our sanity as creatures, a part of the geography of hope."[3] Such a seamless identification of wilderness with sanity and hope could only have emerged from a posture toward the world as cosmos—an ordered whole brought into existence by a God who is good.

To put my thesis in its simplest terms: the Wilderness Act and the overall movement of environmental concern out of which it came is rooted in the unexpressed but nonetheless unequivocal affirmation that creation is good

---

2 The Wilderness Act of 1964, Pub. L. No. 88–577, 78 Stat. 890 (1964), accessed at https://wilderness.nps.gov/document/wildernessAct.pdf.

3 Wallace Stegner, *The Sound of Mountain Water: The Changing American West* (London: Penguin Books, 1980), 115.

and that it is an intrinsic value to be shared, that nature in its vastness offers something worthy to behold. The opportunity to behold it, to stand before its veiled splendor, is an essential element of our human, our religious, our national flourishing. Ours will forever remain a religious nation as long as our natural piety is preserved and the porticoes of the sacred—that is, our wilderness spaces— remain open to its citizens.

The Wilderness Act is a miraculous achievement on the part of the American people who put into practice the theological conviction that creation is good—indeed, very good. As the Lord employed Cyrus in order to achieve his aims in restoring Jerusalem (as noted by the prophet Isaiah), He used the Johnson administration in a kind of modern day equivalent. For through Him (and others engaged in similar efforts) the foundations were laid for the rebuilding of a renewed Jerusalem, a Christian culture which can only be built upon the pillars of the earth, can only be built from the ground up. And so my effort is not a call to some kind of back-to-nature movement or an altar call to a nature cult.

These remarks should be taken as a foreword (really, a plea and a prayer) for a much deeper and profound revolution: to set in motion the conditions in which a renewed, authentic Catholic culture can emerge. For here and only here, squarely within this temple of creation, a Catholic culture takes root: the good news of Jesus Christ moves from its conceptual power to its cultural expression; heaven and earth are wed in the physical body of the believer, the mystical body of believers; and the plan of the Incarnation takes root in history.

Announcing this gospel of creation can once again place our lives at the service of humanity and allow us to be that *lumen gentium*, a light to peoples who are currently mesmerized by the environmental movement. In some ways, the movement is a revolt of conscience among those generations of postmodernity who have sensed that something is deeply flawed in our stance before the natural order, that the habit of treating creatures as a raw datum of purposeless stuff is not consonant with reality. In deeper ways, the movement expresses the deep-seated, felt need across cultures and traditions to connect with the earth and assume a peaceful place within it. The recent work of ecopsychologists affirms the value of encountering nature and coming into contact more intentionally with one's natural surroundings. The work of Richard Louv and others, recognizing the "nature-deficit disorder" that plagues so much of modern living, argues that substantial empirical evidence exists that shows exposure to our natural surroundings brings significant health benefits.[4]

Green Thomists seek to contribute to this culture of integral ecology in order to accompany modern pilgrims in their quest for self-transcendence, much the same way as Francis invites the world, through *Laudato si'*, to develop an integral ecology for the sake of a deeper encounter with Christ. Of course the search is as varied as the searchers that undertake it, and not every occasion of encounter is an experience of mutual evangelization. But confidence in the Logos and the Spirit which proceeds demands that we

---

[4] Richard Louv, *The Nature Principle: Reconnecting with Life in a Virtual Age* (Chapel Hill, NC: Algonquin Books of Chapel Hill, 2012), 58.

take the best of our neighbors' intentions and aspirations and accompany them on their journey toward fulfillment.

No discussion of integral ecology, however, can ignore the fact that "nature"—verdant pastures, sylvan glens, meandering streams, and hills dusted in the chartreuse of early spring—also means death. It may be popular to talk about the green movement; it could just as accurately be described as the brown movement. Nature, Aristotle reminds us, is a principle of change—and change means the coming of things to be *and* their passing. It is important to recall that the circle of life includes the cycle of death.

A spirituality that seeks an integral life demands developing a keener insight into the reality of death and its significance. Death, for the Christian, is bound up with the question of sin, and it will therefore be necessary to turn attention to the issues surrounding sin and the place of the human person within the drama of sin and redemption. The inspired author of Ecclesiastes captures it:

> I said in my heart with regard to the sons of men that God is testing them to show them that they are but beasts. For the fate of the sons of men and the fate of beasts is the same; as one dies, so dies the other. They all have the same breath, and man has no advantage over the beasts; for all is vanity. All go to one place; all are from the dust, and all turn to dust again. Who knows whether the spirit of man goes upward and the spirit of the beast goes down to the earth? (Eccl 3:18–21)

Ecclesiastes offers a poignant perspective that many of us, including faithful men and women, can sometimes adopt when we consider the fate of animals, indeed all creatures, including ourselves. Death seems to be the final arbiter and its universal law seems to nullify any sense of a unique purpose, especially to something as trivial as ecology when viewed from the cold horizon of evolution and death.

Good men and women are vulnerable to the pressures of contemporary philosophies, which have denuded the natural order of any supernatural significance, erasing the handwriting of God and reducing nature to essentially a blank slate upon which we moderns could then write our own script. The critique of such philosophies and their impact on attitudes towards nature is familiar and need not be repeated here.

But a certain degree of confusion that is prevalent within Christian circles makes discerning the basic outlines of an integral ecology especially difficult. Here the confusion is due not so much to alien philosophies of nature but rather to confusion concerning some principles of Christian anthropology. Chief among the sources of confusion within the faithful is the matter of original sin.

Now is not the time to review its doctrinal status in the tradition. Suffice it to say that the *Catechism of the Catholic Church* speaks of original sin as "an essential doctrine of the Christian faith." Describing it in terms of "original" points us back to the origins of the human condition as well as ahead to the systemic impact of its consequences for us now. Like the notion of "primitive" in the discussion of awe in the prior chapter, "original" has the sense of historic priority, but experiential priority as well. Original sin inescapably colors experience, including my experience of nature, and so a keener awareness of its debilitating effects is a necessary step in developing an integral, spiritually sound ecology.

> What Revelation makes known to us is confirmed by our own experience. For when man looks into his own heart he finds that he is drawn toward what is wrong and sunk in many evils which cannot come from his good creator. Often refusing to acknowledge God as his source, man has also upset the relationship which should link him to his last end; and at the same time he has broken the right order that should reign within himself, as well as between himself and other men and all creatures.[5]

Note the three kinds of relationships that *Gaudium et Spes* says are marred by original sin, the fundamental refusal to acknowledge God as source and end.

The first consequence pertains to disquietude in the interior life, the inability to love and do the good with any degree of consistency. St. Paul speaks eloquently about the experience of a "war within his members" which keeps him from doing what he knows to be good and avoiding that which he knows is evil (Rom 7:15). "Concupiscence" is the general title given to those persistent and unruly impulses toward self-centeredness which constantly lurk in the recesses of human motivations and actions and against

---

[5] *Gaudium et Spes*, 13.1.

which we must do constant battle. Countless volumes have been written on the subject through the centuries.

The second fracture traces the lines of the relationships we share with each other: not only as social creatures are we now mired in the habits of injustice and inequity, but as sexual creatures in relationship with other men or women, the *libido dominandi*, the desire to dominate, persistently overwhelms better judgments. St. John Paul II's extensive meditations on the theology of the body and the general literature surrounding the complementarity of the sexes come to mind here when thinking about the extensive teachings on the matter.

The third rupture in experience pertains to our relationship with other creatures. It is no less colored by the effects of original sin, but by comparison, this arena has received significantly less attention. It is primarily this third arena—our relationships within the rest of creation, the animated communities to which we belong as embodied, spiritual creatures of the earth, that is, the creaturely world that comprises our environment—which is the special focus here.

In this regard, significantly less has been written and the Catholic theological community may be rightly described as behind the curve on these theological aspects of the environment. *Laudato si'*, written just in these past few years, corrects the dramatic lacunae in the Church's magisterium, if only to confirm the rule by proving the exception. Prior to its pronouncement by Pope Francis, no pope had taken on the subject as directly as he had in this groundbreaking encyclical. St. John Paul II and Pope Benedict XVI, "the green pope," began to engage the conversation, but it is fair to say that Pope Francis is to get credit for the truly inspired decision to address the question of the environment directly from a Catholic theological perspective.

I have already stated that some of the reluctance on the part of the Catholic community to engage the questions of ecology is due to the widespread reticence to speak of "humans and their environment," as the language lends itself to certain kinds of humanist or materialistic reductionisms that are simply not consonant with the received tradition. I have also alluded, although briefly, to the problems of Enlightenment philosophies that tended to view nature less from the perspective of its origins in the Logos, or Wisdom of God, and more along the lines of a nexus of mechanistic causes, fully capable of being understood independently of any appeals to theological convictions or attitudes. The perspective dominates the empirical sciences today, which, while not in itself a problem concerning methodologies, can quickly become a problem when such perspectives overreach their competencies and thus morph into ideologies. The matter is poignantly raised, again, by Pope Francis in *Laudato si'* when he speaks of the problems associated with the "technological paradigm." [6]

But there is a deeper dimension to the doctrine of original sin and the challenge of integral ecology which is more poignant, for it eludes many of us in the best theological, ethical, and pastoral circles: the theology of the preternatural gifts and their loss due to original sin.

[6] *LS*, no. 108

Few contemporary Catholics are familiar with the language as it has fallen out of favor in more recent articulations of the faith, but I am persuaded that a reconsideration of their implications can help us gain a better understanding of our place within the natural order and our vocation to steward the goods of the earth as faithful sons and daughters of Christ. It is a matter for dogmatic theologians and Church historians to place the doctrine adequately within the patrimony of the Church. For my purposes, I wish to reflect on their ethical significance for living an integral, ecologically-minded life with Christ.

Allowing for some variation in language, the tradition identifies three preternatural gifts belonging to Adam and Eve prior to the Fall: the gift of integrity, of immortality, and infused knowledge. They are "preternatural" in part to distinguish them from "supernatural gifts," which are bestowed alone by Christ Himself and elevate the soul, especially enabling it to fully partake in the divine nature in eternal beatitude at the end of the world. They are "gifts" in that they exceed the capacity of the human person considered in his or her mere natural condition as such: an animal endowed with a rational soul. In the state of original justice, Adam and Eve enjoy the preternatural gifts of integrity, immortality, and infused knowledge of creation.

In contrast to the "prelapsarian" or pre-fallen condition of original justice, you and I now live under the pall of original sin, the impact of which is impossible to overestimate, though it is always important to remember the remedy: Baptism into Jesus Christ, which is easy to underestimate.

CONCERNING INTEGRITY

In the state of original justice, Adam and Eve enjoyed a life of personal integrity, meaning their feelings and emotions were spontaneously ordered by their intelligence, which was consistently ordered to God. The soul's higher powers of intellect and will exercised authority over their passions as their entire lives were oriented to the goodness of God their Creator. They could make decisions and discern life's choices unencumbered by inordinate fear or anxiety. They enjoyed the freedom of one disciplined in the school of love and truth. Though you and I may now long for a peaceful life of focused commitment to the good, the true, and the beautiful, because of original sin, each one of us is a cauldron of illicit loves (to parse St. Augustine), a witless pastiche of various motives—sometimes virtuous, mostly selfish—moments of half-insight interrupted with outbursts of self-aggrandizement, the private heart more bitter than the public self which surrounds it. Tossed between the Scylla of boredom and the Charybdis of anxiety, the happy life of spontaneous virtue, the consistent freedom to love and do what one wills, to live the God-centered life, is no longer available.

IMMORTALITY

As the very term suggests, the preternatural gift of immortality states that prior to the Fall, Adam and Eve were not subject to the cruelest logic of organic creatures within the natural world: bodily death. But their immunity was not due to any natural condition on their part; rather, it was a special grace, a preternatural gift, which preserved them from the fate of every animal—death. St. Thomas is explicit in his exposition of the faith that while the human soul may surpass the conditions of materiality and thus in one sense be immune from decay, the human body, strictly speaking, is not of itself apt for immortality.

St. Thomas asserts:

> For man's body was indissoluble not by reason of any intrinsic vigor of immortality, but by reason of a supernatural force given by God to the soul, whereby it was enabled to preserve the body from all corruption so long as it remained itself subject to God. This entirely agrees with reason; for since the rational soul surpasses the capacity of corporeal matter, as above explained, it was most properly endowed at the beginning with the power of preserving the body in a manner surpassing the capacity of corporeal matter.[7]

A special preternatural gift of immortality needed to be given to Adam and Eve on account of the fact that they were unique creatures, rational creatures united to organic bodies. And it is this latter condition of organic embodiment that meant they needed some additional grace in escaping the law of organicity: namely, bodily death.

From the perspective of their animality, Adam and Eve should have been subject to the conditions of every animal in the order of creation. But because they were uniquely constituted animals—as creatures who were given the preternatural grace of immortality—they were

[7] *ST* I 97.1.

immune from the inevitability of bodily death.[8] It is this immunity that was subsequently lost in the Fall of Adam and Eve. As St. Thomas says in his *Compendium*,

> Accordingly, if we regard the nature of the body, death is natural. But if we regard the nature of the soul and the disposition with which the human body was supernaturally endowed in the beginning for the sake of the soul, death is *per accidens* and contrary to nature, inasmuch as union with the body is natural for the soul.[9]

It is crucial to comprehend the significance of this thesis for understanding the place of the embodied person as a substantial, organic creature within a material universe. The theology of the preternatural gift of immortality affirms what ordinary experience tells us: animals die and their deaths are part of the ordinary course of events. The world of living creatures is dominated by principles of endurance *and* change, of life *and* death, of green movements *and* brown movements. And because human beings are citizens of this same world, it only stands to reason that we, too, ought to be subject to the same "law of organicity"; we, too, ought to submit to the logic of death. Vanity of vanities!

But Adam and Eve are no ordinary animals. As embodied creatures gifted with the preternatural grace of

---

[8] *ST* I 97.1; *ST* III 14.3 ad 2; *SCG* IV, 81.1; also, *Compendium theologiae ad fratrem Reginaldum socium suum carissimum*, 152; 193.

[9] *Compendium*, 152.

immortality, they escaped the condition of all the en-fleshed—namely, death. Immune from the logic of or-ganic embodied beings, preserved from the vicissitudes of animal existence, unencumbered by the threat of bodily death or decay, they enjoyed not merely the status of a rational animal, but the status of immortal ones.

Until original sin. Due to the cataclysm of original sin, our rational abilities are now wounded, our hearts disordered, our passions set in disarray; but even more significantly, our privilege as immortal animals has been forfeited entirely—"For the wages of sin is death" (Rom 6:23). Now, even the saints have to endure the final tra-vail. In this life, under the curse, if not the torments of an interior sort, then exterior torments abound. So much anxiety arising from the fragility of the flesh, endless preoccupations avoiding the inescapable, glacial grind of bodily entropy, suffering, and death—the cruelest cut of all. For the moment, I am a temporary amalgam of loosely assembled parts, each one poised for war with the elemental forces which surround it, only for the moment suspended above the fray in an uneasy truce called health. With each birthday comes the humble reminder that I stand before my body as an inn-keeper of an unruly mob, beset by the outbursts sounding the various apartments, anxious to keep the disturbances under control, too fearful of the day they decide to check out en masse. In so many ways, and in the most poignant of details, "All go to one place; all are from the dust, and all turn to dust again" (Eccl 3:20). Vanity of vanities, indeed.

Thanks be to God! Christ not only usurps the logic of death and restores the conditions of bodily immortality, but He achieves so much more (Rom 5) than Adam and Eve could ever have accomplished on their own: He clothes us in the garments of adopted children of the Father, and through His Spirit dwells within the soul as divine guest and friend. The black and white world of immortality is transformed into the technicolor kingdom of beatitude, and death becomes the gateway to life.

In Christ, in other words, not only is the punishment for the loss of the preternatural gift of immorality finally undone, but our status before God will exceed what Adam and Eve could ever have known. "The promised reward of the immortality of glory," St. Thomas confirms, "differs from the immortality which was bestowed on man in the state of innocence."[10] The "much more" of Romans 5 points to this divinely granted promotion in status, from stewards of the earth to adopted sons and daughters of its maker.

"O Happy Fault!" the deacon intones in the Exultet at every Easter Vigil, "that earned so great, so glorious a Redeemer," for it was through taking on the punishment of sinful Adam, that Christ has won for us an even more glorious place in heaven. It is the core of the Christian kerygma, the foundation of faith.

What could all of this have to do with developing an integral ecology?

First, Thomas' account of the preternatural gift of immortality points to a decisive conclusion: the deaths of the other animals would have occurred in the prelapsarian state and their deaths would not then (and do not now) directly follow from any particular consequence of orig-

---

[10] *ST* I 97.1 ad 4.

inal sin in the world. The natural deaths of non-human animals, though considered a kind of privation due to the loss of the good of life, is part of the Provident arrangement of things, and is not in itself a manifest effect of sin.[11] It is only when the decimation of creatures is due to some inordinate action on the part of human beings that the question of sin becomes pertinent. Barring such inordinate action, the passing of creatures, however dramatic the scale, remains part of the Provident plan and is only to be an occasion of reflection, not reparation.

It is very popular today to speak as if no death of any creature would have occurred had the drama of original sin never taken place, that carnivores would have changed their ways and adopted vegetarian diets in lieu of a supposed peaceable kingdom. But in St. Thomas' account of things such a worldview is *"omnino irrationabile"*[12]—altogether irrational and is therefore to be summarily dismissed.

It is irrational, St. Thomas believes, because it is contrary to the nature of animals to abandon their animal ways. Predators demand the presence of the predated and such an order reflects the Divine arrangement. "For many good things would be taken away if God permitted no evil to exist; for fire would not be generated if air was not corrupted, nor would the life of a lion be preserved

---

[11] *ST* I 48 2 ad 3. I use "sin" here in the sense of a human or voluntary action not in accord with the order of reason and the Eternal Law. While St. Thomas will speak of monstrosities in nature as a kind of sin (*ST* I-II 21.1 ad 1), this is to be taken in the broadest sense of any action (voluntary or otherwise) lacking due order to its end.

[12] *ST* I. 96.1 ad 2.

unless the ass were killed."[13] His utter confidence in the normative order of nature as given in ordinary experience is the foundational feature of his thought and forms the bedrock of his theological vision of life.[14] In this case especially, it provides the hermeneutic for his account of the prelapsarian state of things.

A second consequence for ecology in Thomas' discussion of the preternatural gifts follows from his exclusive emphasis on the human being in the drama of creation and sin. The non-human, organic world of animated creatures occupies no such special status in the drama. Only the rational creatures—more specifically, the humans—are central characters in the story of the dread of sin and the mercy of God.[15]

From this we learn that protology (the study of origins) is not soteriology (the study of salvation); to be created is not the sufficient condition for being a candidate for redemption. A theology of creation is one thing, and its sheer scope would need to include in its account the glorious non-rational creatures in their every manner of existence. But to introduce the features of sin and its merciful remedy is another facet altogether and focuses the spotlight only on a selected cast of characters, those intellectual creatures endowed with the power of deliberative choice.

---

[13] *ST* I 48.2 ad 3.

[14] For a compelling synopsis of the normative vision of creation, see Steven A. Long, "The Teleological Grammar of the Created Order in Catholic Moral Discourse," in *On Earth as It Is in Heaven: Cultivating a Contemporary Theology of Creation*, ed. David V. Meconi, S.J. (Grand Rapids, MI: Eerdmans, 2016), 37–55.

[15] Still another reason not to envy the angels: the fallen have no hope of expiation (*SCG* IV 55,7).

None of this is meant to dismiss the creature's standing. If anything, Green Thomists are determined to defend it properly. To distinguish is not to divide and certainly not a warrant for domination. All creatures are created by God; each one is willed into existence; each is a reflection of the Trinity;[16] and each one is the caress of Divine Wisdom itself.[17] Animals in particular manifest one of the most glorious facets of the Divine presence in the world—but a facet only, not a face. That privilege is reserved for us alone, who now as living Christs have the vocation to bear His image from here to eternity.[18]

St. Thomas unequivocally affirms that beside their mere status in a "supporting role" in the drama of salvation, "all natural things were produced by the Divine art, and so may be called God's works of art."[19] The corruption of original sin does not penetrate to the lower ranks of creation, for the natures of animals, Thomas says explicitly, were not changed by man's sin.[20] Their habits of being are precisely now what they would have been prior to any fall; for it is only the intellectual creatures (the angels and humans) who are directly caught up in the drama of sin. It is not unfair to suggest here that Thomas' entire treatment of the preternatural gifts is due, in part, to his indefatiga-

---

[16] *ST* I 45.7.

[17] *LS*, no. 84

[18] For an example of a critique of this kind of hierarchical thinking from an eco-feminist perspective, see Laura Hobgood-Oster, *Holy Dogs & Asses: Animals in the Christian Tradition* (Urbana, IL: University of Illinois Press, 2008); also, Elizabeth A. Johnson, *Ask the Beasts: Darwin and the God of Love* (London: Bloomsbury Publishing Place, 2014).

[19] *ST* I 91.3.

[20] *ST* I 96.1 ad 2.

ble defense of the integral gift that is lower creation.

One can only imagine what impact this vision might have in the broader considerations of ecological concern when it comes to be fully understood that the passing away of creatures, perhaps even entire species, may reflect the provident arrangement of things. At issue is the reason for the loss and whether it is due to some inordinate action on the part of reckless human living. But the fact of such loss is a feature of organic life and is the expression of Divine Providence at work. Such events are consistent with the state of original justice and continue in this life in accordance with Divine wisdom.[21]

Integral ecology means that we cannot look upon the natural deaths of creatures and the deaths of human persons in the same light. Their deaths, at least in many cases, positively manifest the Provident order of things; our deaths, on the other hand, are always the regrettable consequence of original sin. Presuming the absence of any disproportionate human acts causing such, a creature's natural death reflects the ordering wisdom of God; our natural death, in contrast, manifests the punishment of sin and points to the need for a Redeemer. Their passing, like all creatures' passing, needs no expiation. The same cannot be said of those fellow human beings who have gone before us, "whose faith and devotion are known to Him alone."[22]

Finally, it should be acknowledged that there are voices in the theological tradition that interpret the status of

---

[21] *ST* I 96.1 ad 2; I 48.2; I 65.1 and 2; I-II 98.4 ad 3.
[22] *Roman Missal*, Eucharistic Prayer I.

animals in the state of original justice differently. Irenaeus of Lyon and Theophilus of Antioch are among some of the earliest defenders of the idea that in the state of original justice, animals behaved differently than what we encounter now. But whatever Paul may have meant by "all creation groaning in travail," Thomas stands with Augustine in his unwillingness to include the plants and animals in Paul's reflection, consistently refusing to bring "lower creation" into the drama of sin and redemption. "Such was the error of the Manichees," Augustine poignantly notes in his *Commentary on Romans*, and Thomas is not about to repeat the mistake.[23]

This is in marked contrast to the widespread scholars who now easily interpret Paul's exhortation in Romans 8:19 to include the ranks of creatures and critters.[24] I suspect it is due to the pastoral urgency we feel in the face of the ecological recklessness we see all about us. But Green Thomists would caution against the overenthusiasm of the age which seeks, out of love for God and creation, to overextend the grace of redemption. We have no memorial Mass for the dinosaurs, nor should we. Like any inordinate love, it would end up destroying the beloved in its anxious grasp. The integrity of creation becomes inadvertently shattered when the drama of redemption is exported to

---

[23] Augustine, *Propositions from the Epistle to the Romans*, 53, in Paula Fredriksen Landes, *Augustine on Romans: Propositions from the Epistle to the Romans; Unfinished Commentary on the Epistle to the Romans* (Chico, CA: Scholars Press, 1982), 23.

[24] Josef A. Fitzmyer, S.J., *Romans: A New Translation With Introduction and Commentary. The Anchor Bible Volume 33* (New York: Doubleday, 1993), 506–509.

its realms. Lower creation is not in need of redemption, for it has never been apt for redemption. The beauty and integrity of the creatures in the cosmos, their pristine conditions of original justice, remain intact and are accessible to this very day. How often eagerness to drag creatures onto the stage of human drama ends in creating monstrosities! Obese, dysmorphic, decrepit, yet oh-so-deeply loved; if only humility would outpace sentimentality, animals just may have a fighting chance at a noble life.

Creatures remain integral; I do not. They dwell in an abyss of light; I live in the darkness of sin. Their intelligibility remains intact;[25] my intelligence is wounded and habitually fraught with error. Their world remains a fertile mystery; my darkened intellect is made brilliant through the inbreak of presence. They spontaneously keep the Divine ways in their comings and goings; my spontaneity is spastic and ordered only occasionally.

I am the steward of the Divine jeweler's shop that is the world, and were I left to my own devices amidst my chronic glaucoma, I would despair at the futility of my effort.

But the event of Christ reminds me that I am no mere steward, but friend, and in that friendship lies the hope for happy stewardship. By grace weakness is healed, humility is strengthened. My care for his cosmos is no longer that of a feeble steward, but an adopted child of the owner. My status is elevated, my defects remedied, and though I may labor with the limits of a dim-witted apprentice, my aims are more modest and thus more noble because they

---

[25] *ST* I-II 98.4 ad 3.

are rightly ordered to the glory of God. For all belongs to me and I belong to Christ and Christ belongs to God (1 Cor 3:21–23).

SELECTED READINGS FOR CHAPTER FIVE

On the Meaning of Action
"Contrary to Reason"

If it belongs to the essence of human reason that the reality of the world as well as of ourselves becomes present and palpable to us only in its light and in no other way; and if, moreover, our reason is not a light that we ignite on our own but is communicated to us, is a participation in that aboriginal light that, as Plato said of the sun, both makes things visible and makes our eyes to see;—then that means, as Aristotle had long ago concluded, that the most decisive characteristic that distinguishes being "in accord with reason" from being "contrary to reason" always depends on whether or not one is directing oneself toward or away from objective reality as well as toward or away from the creative Logos that manifests itself to us in our own power of cognition.

—Josef Pieper, *The Concept of Sin*
(South Bend, IN: St. Augustine's Press, 2001), 49–50

On Certain Implications Concerning the
Loss of Original Justice

The harmonious integrity of the original state depended entirely on the submission of man's will to God. Consequently, as soon as the human will threw off the yoke of subjection to God, the perfect subjection of the lower powers to reason and of the body to the soul likewise disintegrated. As a result, man experienced in his lower, sensitive appetite the inordinate stirrings of concupiscence, anger, and all the other passions. These movements no longer followed the order set by reason but rather resisted reason, frequently darkening the mind, and so to speak, throwing it into confusion. This is the rebellion of the flesh that Scripture mentions. . . . A further consequence was that the defect which consists in corruption was experienced in the body, and so man incurred the necessity of dying; his soul was no longer able to sustain the body forever conferring life on it. Thus man became subject to suffering and death, not only in the sense that he was capable of suffering and dying as before, but in the sense that he was now under the necessity of suffering and dying.

—St. Thomas Aquinas, *Light of Faith: The Compendium of Theology*
(Manchester, NH: Sophia Institute Press, 2003), sections 192–93

On the Demands of Christian Spirituality

Christian spirituality proposes an alternative understanding of the quality of life, and encourages a prophetic and contemplative lifestyle, one capable of deep enjoyment free of the obsession with consumption. We need to take up an ancient lesson, found in different religious traditions and also in the Bible. It is the conviction that "less is more." A constant flood of new consumer goods can baffle the heart and prevent us from cherishing each thing and each moment. To be serenely present to each reality, however small it may be, opens us to much greater horizons of understanding and personal fulfillment. Christian spirituality proposes a growth marked by moderation and the capacity to be happy with little. It is a return to that simplicity which allows us to stop and appreciate the small things, to be grateful for the opportunities which life affords us, to be spiritually detached from what we possess, and not to succumb to sadness for what we lack. This implies avoiding the dynamic of dominion and the mere accumulation of pleasures.

Such sobriety, when lived freely and consciously, is liberating. It is not a lesser life or one lived with less intensity. On the contrary, it is a way of living life to the full. In reality, those who enjoy more and live better each moment are those who have given up dipping here and there, always on the look-out for what they do not have. They experience what it means to appreciate each person and each thing, learning familiarity with the simplest things and how to enjoy them. So they are able to shed unsatisfied needs, reducing their obsessiveness and weariness. Even living on little, they can live a lot, above all when they cultivate other pleasures and find satisfaction in fraternal encounters, in service, in developing their gifts, in music and art, in contact with nature, in prayer. Happiness means knowing how to limit some needs which only diminish us, and being open to the many different possibilities which life can offer.

Sobriety and humility were not favorably regarded in the last century. And yet, when there is a general breakdown in the exercise of a certain virtue in personal and social life, it ends up causing a number of imbalances, including environmental ones. That is why it is no longer enough to speak only of the integrity of ecosystems. We have to dare to speak of the integrity of human life, of the need to promote and unify all the great values. Once we lose our humility, and become enthralled with the possibility of limitless mastery over everything, we inevitably end up harming society and the environment. It is not easy to promote this kind of healthy humility or happy sobriety when we consider ourselves autonomous, when we exclude God from our lives or replace Him with our own ego, and think that our subjective feelings can define what is right and what is wrong.

—Pope Francis, *LS*, no. 222–224

SELECTED RESOURCES FOR CHAPTER FIVE

Josef Cardinal Ratzinger, *'In the Beginning. . .': A Catholic Understanding of the Story of Creation and the Fall*, trans. Boniface Ramsey, O.P. (Grand Rapids, MI: Eerdmans, 1986).

Josef Pieper, *The Concept of Sin*, trans. Edward T. Oakes, S.J. (South Bend, IN: St. Augustine's Press, 2001).

·⟡·

CHAPTER SIX

The Fragile Gift of Creation

"All natural things were produced by the Divine art, and so may be called God's works of art."[1]

WE ought to linger a bit in the prelapsarian world and garner a few more insights before venturing into the challenge of pursuing an integral, ecologically-sound spirituality in this "valley of tears." St. Thomas spends not a few articles in the *Summa* discussing our unique condition in this state. Quaint in many ways as compared to more sophisticated expectations of theological scholarship, the discussion nonetheless highlights crucial elements.

For through all of his attention to detail, a certain logic predominates: everything created by God is good and reflects the divine wisdom in its order and aims. Each living creature bears the trace of the divine and participates in that goodness to the extent to which it is capable. The human person alone bears the *imago Dei*, as a creature endowed with intellect and will, and this fact will mark

[1] *ST* I 91.3.

the privilege of the human creature within the universe. But this is not the whole story of creation, sin, and redemption. Because the other creatures of "lower creation" are immune to the drama of sin and redemption, we can remain confident today that their narrative continues to speak directly of the glory of God. And thus, "When I behold the heavens, the works of your hands, the moon and the stars which you have made"... I, with the Psalmist, embark upon an interior dialogue with the Logos of Creation, a prayer repeated in the hearts of a thousand generations, as each human being contemplates the wonders of the universe, its splendor, its gift, its meaning and ours within it. Mary Oliver reminds us,

> Whoever you are, no matter how lonely,
> the world offers itself to your imagination,
> calls to you like the wild geese, harsh and exciting
> over and over announcing your place
> in the family of things.[2]

Adam, the *imago*, had the privilege of contemplating the universe in the very company of its maker, "walking in the garden in the cool of the day" (Gen 3:8). Undimmed by ignorance and self-centeredness, Adam could linger among the gifts of God, and in the midst of the family of things, spontaneously turn his mind to God's truth, his heart to God's goodness. The experience of awe before the beauty of creation in this condition was his by hab-

---

[2] Mary Oliver, "Wild Geese," in *Dream Work* (New York: Atlantic Monthly Press, 1986), 14.

it and marked a posture of prayer and praise before the beauty of the world. "Through the intelligible effects of God, man [before the Fall] knew God then more clearly," Thomas says, "than we know Him now."[3]

Such peaceful sympathies were occasioned not merely with outward considerations, but also within his interior life, for this, too, reflected the Divine ordering at work. His passions and emotions, his experiences and insights, his camaraderie with Eve, all unencumbered by sin! Their bodies in particular bore the signs of companionship as they enjoyed the company of each other in friendship, in flesh. His knowledge of all other things was by divine infusion, as opposed to us who must now learn through fits and starts, the school of hard knocks, experience. Still, the content was much the same, it would seem, "for [Adam's] knowledge was not different from ours; as the eyes which Christ gave to the man born blind were not different from those given by nature."[4]

As far as his feelings were concerned, his passions were similar to ours with respect to the good things of life and their due order: love and delight, desire and hope. The feelings of dread or despair, however, were absent his days, as the evil from which they emerge has not yet come on the scene. Inordinate desire for sex, too, was foreign to them both, "for in that state, fecundity would have been without lust."[5] "Rather, in the state of innocence," Thomas says, "the inferior appetite was wholly subject to reason:

---

[3] *ST* I 94.1.
[4] *ST* I 94.3 ad 1.
[5] *ST* I 98.2 ad 3.

so that in that state the passions of the soul existed only as consequent upon the judgment of reason."[6] Reason is not the enemy of intense pleasure, only disordered pleasure.

Now under the shadow of original sin, however, the matter is different. "For our sensual appetite, wherein the passions reside, is not entirely subject to reason; hence at times our passions forestall and hinder reason's judgment; at other times they follow reason's judgment, accordingly as the sensual appetite obeys reason to some extent."[7] As Gerard Manley Hopkins, S.J., eloquently puts it,

> . . . Oh, the sots and thralls of lust
> Do in spare hours more thrive than I that spend,
> Sir, life upon thy cause.[8]

As the *imago Dei*, we participate in a wonderfully ordered cosmos with unique features that reflect this privileged status: the powers of understanding and choosing. These intellectual capacities of intellect and will, nonetheless, are inescapably dependent upon our animal-like senses. For St. Thomas, there is nothing in the intellect that is not first presented through the senses. All of the content of our thinking begins in our embodied, sensual experience of the world. We need to see, hear, feel, smell, and taste the character of things before we can imagine, ponder, reflect, consider, and decide their significance.

---

[6] *ST* I 95.2.

[7] Ibid.

[8] Gerard Manley Hopkins, S.J., "Thou art indeed just, Lord, if I contend," Lord, if I contend" in Gerard Manley Hopkins, *Poems and Prose*, ed. W. H. Gardner. (London: Penguin Classics, 1985), 67.

Feelings and emotions, too, taking their cue from the content of our thoughts, are indirectly dependent upon the package of sense data, "the experience," that enters our consciousness through the body. In the genesis of our ideas, the order of causality is "from the ground up," if you will, from the data of the senses to the consideration of the intellect, from the world of sensual episodes into the brilliant world of meaning in motion.

In the prelapsarian state, because Adam and Eve enjoyed an unmitigated health and wellness, the movement from the sheer stuff of the world to the world of meaning, truth, and love was unencumbered by the disordering of sin within their souls.

But even in their state of bliss, it was not all a matter of sensual causes followed by intellectual effects. In the enactment of ideas, the living out of insights and aspirations now shaped through experience, the ordering is reversed; it flows "from the top down," or from the inward to the outward. The intellect seizes on an insight and offers to the will a good to be pursued. Together, the two powers give birth to the human choice and begin to set a meaning into motion. The polarity is reversed to a certain extent as the body responds to the commands of the will, enlightened by the truth of things, and life becomes a plan of harmony, a dialectic of illuminating experience culminating in deliberative joy.

Now, after the Fall, the matter is entirely different and demands a certain precision of analysis. The disorder of sin impacts primarily the "core powers" of intellect and will. The spontaneous exercise of command and control of one's coming and going, once an effortless expression of love and truth, is weakened in its core and spreads through the operations of the human psyche, beginning primarily in the will—which no longer submits exclusively to the truth of things, no longer pursues the good with any degree of consistency. Instead, it yields to the strong desires for pleasure, with no regard for the overall health of the body, the well-being of one's neighbors, or the fellow creatures with which one shares the earth. The disordering spreads from the inner regions outward, from the intimate facets of the interior life to its outward expression in action and enactment. Or as Thomas expresses it: "A sinful defect may be transferred from the soul to the body, but not conversely, for we call something sinful according as there is a de-ordination of the will."[9]

Strictly speaking, the functioning of the senses remains intact (save for the occasion of bodily illness or defect) and the experiences of pleasure and pain—at the most rudimentary, biological level—continue to reflect the divine ordering at work.[10] Where the dysfunction occurs is in the reception of that data and the transformation of that data into action. Certain values and valuations now reflect a disordered predilection, the reception of certain truths of things takes on a ranking of its own. One can still hear just fine; it is just that one no longer cares to listen. One's vision may be 20/20, but the will to see is not there. What was once a source of unmitigated truth, namely, the experience of things, is now qualified in its value as it is no longer received as "truth." My will begins

[9] *SCG* III 127, 4.
[10] *ST* I-II 106.3 ad 3.

to bend my experiences according to its own fancies, particularly its own self-love, and thus my "experience" of the world is now entangled in "internal politics" if you will. Over time, certain pleasures morph from the occasional event to a persistent habit and, depending upon the intensity of the pleasure under consideration, form a seemingly inescapable chain that enslaves the person in their own menagerie of delusions.

The problem lies not in the mechanics of the body and its sense experiences, as such, but rather in the valuations we now ascribe to these data. From our very origins now, we put the individual self above the needs of others, the part of pleasure above the integrity of the whole truth, the short-term gain for the longer horizon, one's pride before one's capacity to love. To put it in terms of this chapter: my insatiable drive to consume over the truth of integral ecology. We have eyes, but we no longer see; we have ears, but we no longer hear.

The body and its functions remain integral after the Fall, and thus disclose the basic features of a moral norm to guide our now poor thinking and self-centered decision making. Nature remains the norm in this sense: that the activity of the body provides something of an outline of the good which is to be pursued and the evils which are to be avoided. The rather familiar profile of hunger, for example, points to the need for nutrition. In turn, the process of digestion illustrates the importance of eating well for the sake of overall health. Sin takes as its starting point the integrity of these processes and twists them to ends which are soon incompatible with one's overall flourishing. Nutrition tends to be co-opted into self-serving aims and my healthy need for nutrition is twisted into gluttony. The sin of gluttony has nothing to do with digestion per se, nor even the desire for food when hungry. The sin lies in my distortion of this value, the ranking of food in a manner discordant with the truth of things. It is my will to self-centeredness which lies at the heart of gluttony, not my body in its natural needs.

In the physical signs of its sexual expression, too, the body remains integral in its functioning. Ordered to the union of a man and a woman and pointing toward the creation of new life, sexual desire for union between the sexes—in itself—remains reflective of the original conditions of sexual communion and friendship. But now sin takes precedence, unfortunately too frequently, and due to the vehemence of the pleasures associated, the once free expression of integral union becomes mired in lust. The free association of a man and a woman united in mutual love and respect, expressed in the sheer delight of intercourse, is now a fleeting fantasy, an image that can either inspire or haunt us depending upon the trajectory of our lives as a journey toward freedom or a spiral into vice.

The human body discloses the moral norms, nonetheless, if only in outline, because "the good of human nature," understood as the principles and powers of the soul in relation to its body, were not destroyed or diminished by sin.[11] It is only to the extent that those powers come under the influence of a weakened will or misguided intellect that such powers become the occasion, not the cause, of unhappiness. The *imago Dei*, the title to which

---

[11] *ST* I-II 85.1; I-II 106.3 ad 3.

we so proudly cling among the creatures of the universe, is also the point of departure for the greatest embarrassments.

The body and its natural functions give us the outlines of moral integrity—but in the way that a photographic negative points to the full picture. Its illuminative power is reversed in the light of authentic moral living. The body and its purposes, in other words, point out to us what ought *not* to be done, what is objectively harmful to the person, contrary to their authentic flourishing, at odds with an integral wellness. The body and its purposes outline the negative norm, that which ought not to be done, that which is *contra naturam*, and thus opposed to God. If the moral life consisted only in the avoidance of evil, the most slavish of physicalisms would suffice. But because we are made not merely to avoid sin, but to love completely—fully, eyes wide, arms open, a symphony of light and life—the powers of intellect and will make their rightful contribution to the glorious rhythms of love, for the body is made for the sake of the soul. The person stamps the impress of character upon their actions through his or her choices in living and is not a mere automaton of the species. The positive aspects of the moral life—eating well, living well, loving well—here the intellect and will, make their legitimate contribution and are welcomed back to the stage of moral drama.

Though weakened by sin, the inclination to virtue on the part of the intellect and will is never totally destroyed. "Even in the lost the natural inclination to virtue remains, else they would have no remorse of conscience. . . . Thus even in a blind man the aptitude to see remains in the very root of his nature in as much as he is an animal naturally endowed with sight."[12] But it is an inclination that is unsteady, uneven in its expression, unguided in its direction. Broken by sin, mired in self-will, blind to the truth of things around me, suspicious of the glory within, I am the captain of a body now too much for me to handle with any degree of success or consistency. But I am a captain, nonetheless, an *imago* to be more precise, and though the title only highlights the humiliating gulf between my standing and my practice, its privilege remains. The medium through which the restoration of my soul—and all those things He places under my care—will find their hope, their redemption, precisely through this blessed body by which I come to know and to love. The wound, it turns out, is precisely the point of His healing touch. God takes on a human body of the earth so that the human body might bear the presence of God on it. Grace perfects our weakened condition and heals what is broken; the deaf begin to hear, the blind begin to see, the lame begin to dance, the ruin of the body is restored into a temple of the Holy Spirit.

Have I strayed from the thesis of integral ecology? Green Thomism would argue we have come to the heart of it. For what else does "integral" mean if not a holistic outlook and practice in the full panoply of choices I face as a graced creature of this glorious earth? Here the fissure in Catholic moral thought is most keenly felt and in desperate need of repair. On the one side stand those who are environmentally aware, keenly attuned to the infractions we enact in relationship with creation and its creatures.

---

[12] *ST* I-II 85.2 ad 3.

On the other are the keepers of Catholic sexual norms. Integral ecology seeks to bridge this divide and recognize that the human person who is tasked with ecology is the same person tasked with chastity and vice versa. The demands are the same in that they all turn upon a respect for creation and the wisdom of the Creator at work in every creature of the earth.

Did Adam (and presumably Eve) have "mastery" over the animals? Yes, St. Thomas says, but not in the manner you and I may be inclined to think. Here Thomas creates a kind of hierarchy of dominion, recognizing that even in the state of innocence, the powers of the human person followed a limiting order. Adam is not to be understood as a character in some fairy tale of sorcery, whereby in the blink of an eye, a rock may be converted to a toad, or a toad to a prince. Instead, the mastery he exercised over other things mirrored the mastery which he was assigned in his own person. As St. Thomas says,

> Man in a certain sense contains all things; and so according as he is master of what is within himself, in the same way he can have mastership over other things. Now we may consider four things in man: his "reason," which makes him like to the angels; his "sensitive powers," whereby he is like the animals; his "natural forces," which liken him to the plants; and "the body itself," wherein he is like to inanimate things. Now in man reason has the position of a master and not of a subject. Wherefore man had no mastership over the angels in the primitive state; so when we read "all creatures,"

we must understand the creatures which are not made to God's image. Over the sensitive powers . . . which obey reason in some degree, the soul has mastership by commanding. So in the state of innocence man had mastership over the animals by commanding them. But of the natural powers and the body itself man is master not by commanding, but by using them. Thus also in the state of innocence man's mastership over plants and inanimate things consisted not in commanding or in changing them, but in making use of them without hindrance.[13]

And so it would seem that "mastery," that is, the capacity to command and direct others, even in the state of innocence, was limited to the animal world. The angelic order was beyond his authority; the plant and organic world, beyond his reach.

Once again, we see a respect in the orders of being and their respective causality the human person, even in the state of innocence, is not quite fully in charge of his universe. The unbridled exercise of power over everything within his grasp may be the dreams of modern man, but it would be a nightmarish scenario for the first family in their circumstances of natural happiness and bliss.

Even the mastery of the animals is unusually curtailed in St. Thomas' account, our relationship being one less of control and manipulation and more that of steward and caretaker. Again, Thomas says,

[13] *ST* I 96.2.

In the state of innocence man would not have had any bodily need of animals—neither for clothing, since then they were naked and not ashamed, there being no inordinate motions of concupiscence—nor for food, since they fed on the trees—nor to carry him about, his body being strong enough for that purpose. But man needed animals in order to have experimental knowledge of their natures. This is signified by the fact that God led the animals to man, that he might give them names expressive of their respective natures.[14]

The world of creatures is not for consumption and most certainly not for exploitation, but is there for the sake of sheer delight in discovering the truth of things. And through this apprenticeship of truth-in-being, one becomes schooled in love, a lover of things, not as one's end, but for the occasion they provide for discovering their source in God, Creator of all creatures, Redeemer of all saved.

To be certain, the search for God is now fraught with error and fragility due to the weakness of our fallen condition, but the overall context of creation and my dignity within it remains intact and forms the fundamental context of a spiritually-enriched integral ecology. The outlook is now as an enlightened steward of the earth (and, through Baptism, a privileged child of the owner of the universe), whose creatures are endowed with the wisdom of God Himself, a wisdom now discerned only in pieces

---

[14] *ST* I 94.1 ad 3.

and in passing, but a wisdom that demands a respect and humility before the creatures of the world. I care for them out of a love for the God who made them, and gave them to me that I might discern in them more readily the wisdom and order of love that lies at the heart of things. They are the first tutors concerning the presence of God, and before their manifest beauty and ordered arrangement I am an eager pupil in the one-room school of the universe.

Throughout St. Thomas' entire discussion of the human being in the state of innocence, it is our human animality, our embodied, located, earthy and earth-conditioned existence which is indefatigably defended. We are spirited creatures apt for God, yet nonetheless yoked to the earth. At no point does the logic of organic existence, our animality, become suspended or dismissed. For to do so would compromise the integrity of created things as given by God in their original condition. We are, as all the animals of the earth, bound by the logic of embodied creatureliness. We eat, we have sex, and yes, we even defecate—none of which reflects the results of some fallenness.[15] Instead, such ways reflect the originative, divinely-ordained conditions of our creatureliness as animals bearing the *imagines Dei* in the glorious cosmos of God. Our animality is the earthen vessel into which the life of grace will eventually be poured, our fleshly life the vessel of our salvation. We occupy the cosmos as a substantial union of soil and spirit. It is our special dignity and it will not be compromised even in the conditions of the new heavens and earth.

[15] *ST* I 97.3 ad 4.

In this meantime, however, after the Fall and before the fulfillment of beatitude, we need to understand more fully the existential condition we find ourselves in as an embodied, rational creature who was once apt for immortality, enjoyed personal integrity, and was fully enlightened by the universe which surrounds us.

Now, we are subject to the logic of death and are disintegrated in the interior life. We grope in ignorance throughout the universe that surrounds us. The sources of brokenness lie not in things, neither in the plants that surround us nor the creatures in all of their excellence. The fissure begins within the mysterious recesses of the soul, the intellect and will, and radiates outward toward a disorder now impressed in the use of things. Even the body, integral in its animality, suffers the loss of original sin "from the top down," if you will, from the intellect and will which exercise a fragile authority over the body, now prone to disruption. It is not the creatures that are sinful, nor the body itself by which we share their environment that is the source of sin. Rather the origins of the spiritual disease lie in our spiritual powers—our intellects now darkened; our wills now weakened.

It is not food itself nor the need for nutrition that is sinful, in other words, because every animal seeks sustenance. Rather, it is the willful desire for excessive food that is the problem, and this is rooted in the refusal to see the truth of things and to follow. It is not the beauty of the universe nor the ability for sight that is disordered, but the inordinate desire to continually seek what is private that makes the custody of the eyes so necessary. It is not the sounds of the earth and its music that is evil, nor the capacity to hear; instead, it is the willful refusal to listen to the truth of others that marks our ways now as self-centered and selfish. It is neither the beauty of the body nor the pleasures of sex that are evil; rather, it is our willful refusal to guide these pleasures along the lines of justice which is the cause of so much heartache in the world.

Developing a keener grasp of the fact that we are wounded amidst an otherwise integral cosmos can help strengthen the resolve to imagine a world in which an integral ecology becomes the first feature of the holy, happy life. In fact, we can perhaps begin to see that "integral ecology" is the foundation for the moral life, since it is within this setting of an integral cosmos, a theonomically ordered universe, that we begin a journey toward healing and recovery, and return to the Father we once knew as friend.

SELECTED READINGS FOR CHAPTER SIX

On Whether Adam in the State of Innocence Had Mastership over the Animals?

In the opinion of some, those animals which now are fierce and kill others, would, in that state, have been tame, not only in regard to man, but also in regard to other animals. But this is quite unreasonable. For the nature of animals was not changed by man's sin, as if those whose nature now it is to devour the flesh of others, would then have lived on herbs, as the lion and falcon. Nor does Bede's gloss on Genesis 1:30 say that trees and herbs were given as food to all animals and birds, but to some. Thus there would have been a natural antipathy between some animals. They would not, however, on this account have been excepted from the mastership of man: as neither at present are they for that reason excepted from the mastership of God, Whose Providence has ordained all this. Of this Providence man would have been the executor, as appears even now in regard to domestic animals, since fowls are given by men as food to the trained falcon.

Reply to Objection 3. In the state of innocence man would not have had any bodily need of animals—neither for clothing, since then they were naked and not ashamed, there being no inordinate motions of concupiscence—nor for food, since they fed on the trees of paradise—nor to carry him about, his body being strong enough for that purpose. But man needed animals in order to have experimental knowledge of their natures. This is signified by the fact that God led the animals to man that he might give them names expressive of their respective natures. . . .

—St. Thomas Aquinas, *ST* I 96.1

On Whether in the State of Innocence There Would Have Been Generation by Coition?

Some of the earlier doctors, considering the nature of concupiscence as regards generation in our present state, concluded that in the state of innocence generation would not have been effected in the same way. Thus Gregory of Nyssa says that in paradise the human race would have been multiplied by some other means. . . . But this is unreasonable. For what is natural to man was neither acquired nor forfeited by sin. Now it is clear that generation by coition is natural to man by reason of his animal life, which he possessed even before sin . . . just as it is natural to other perfect animals, as the corporeal members make it clear.

—St. Thomas Aquinas, *ST* I 98.2

On the Ecology of the Human Body

Human ecology also implies another profound reality: the relationship between human life and the moral law, which is inscribed in our nature and is necessary for the creation of a more dignified environment. Pope Benedict XVI spoke of an "ecology of man," based on the fact that "man too has a nature that he must respect and that he cannot manipulate at will." It is enough to recognize that our body itself establishes us in a direct relationship with the environment and with other living beings. The acceptance of our bodies as God's gift is vital for welcoming and accepting the entire world as a gift from the Father and our common home, whereas thinking that we enjoy absolute power over our own bodies turns, often subtly, into thinking that we enjoy absolute power over creation. Learning to accept our body, to care for it and to respect its fullest meaning, is an essential element of any genuine human ecology. Also, valuing one's own body in its femininity or masculinity is necessary if I am going to be able to recognize myself in an encounter with someone who is different. In this way we can joyfully accept the specific gifts of another man or woman, the work of God the Creator, and find mutual enrichment. It is not a healthy attitude which would seek "to cancel out sexual difference because it no longer knows how to confront it."

—Pope Francis, *LS*, no. 155

SELECTED RESOURCES FOR CHAPTER SIX

The Catechism of the Catholic Church, Second Edition (Vatican City: Libreria Editrice Vaticana, 1997), nos. 385–412.

The International Theological Commission, *Communion and Stewardship: Human Persons Created in the Image of God* (Vatican City: Libreria Editrice Vaticana, 2004).

Pontifical Council for Justice and Peace, *Compendium of the Social Doctrine of the Church* (Vatican City: Libreria Editrice Vaticana, 2004), Chapter 10, "Safeguarding the Environment."

·❋·

CHAPTER SEVEN

CONTRA MUNDUM; SECUNDUM NATURAM

"If creatures withdraw us from God, it is the fault of those who use them foolishly."[1]

Contra mundum, secundum naturam, ad maiorem dei gloriam!

THAT is the mantra of integral ecology: to live one's life resisting worldliness, according to one's nature (and dignity), for the greater glory of God.

"Worldliness," in this instance, is that realm of relationships impacted by sin. It is that order of relationships about which the First Letter of John speaks so starkly: "Do not love the world or the things in the world. If anyone loves the world, love for the Father is not in him. For all that is in the world, the lust of the flesh and the lust of the eyes and the pride of life, is not of the Father but is of the world" (1 Jn 2:15–16). Here "the world" is the sum total of wicked ways and their implications beyond us: the

---

[1] *ST* I 65.1 ad 3.

inordinate lust of the flesh seen in the effects of excessive consumption; the lust of the eyes in the salacious conquest of nature; the pride of life which constantly puts one's own needs before the needs of other creatures and neighbors; the lack of regard for the circumstances of others; the contempt for the environment and its inhabitants; a nonchalance of indifference for God and His creatures. It is a kind of systemic corruption of living experience and as such is "a world" that we are to make every effort to resist. Like ripples on the water's surface shattered by a stone, the effect of original sin spreads in concentric circles outward from the darkened recesses of the wounded soul to "the world," setting in motion the most dramatic of climate changes.

But the more remote one gets from the heart of the disturbance, the closer one can discern the original wisdom in things. "Nature" is the norm in a theonomic universe, and familiarity with its ways is an apprenticeship in the Wisdom of God. Indeed, the very definition of sin handed on through the centuries was the notion of a deliberate act which is "*contra naturam*," or contrary to the nature of the human person as created. St. Thomas states it plainly: "Wherefore in sins contrary to nature, whereby the very order of nature is violated, an injury is done to God, the author of nature."[2]

Living a life "*secundum naturam*" means living in accordance with the dignity of one's nature and acknowledging the divine order written in the structure of things, things of the simplest magnitude, things of dramatic significance. While one can never forget that human nature and animal

---

[2] *ST* I-II 154.12 ad 1.

natures differ in kind in matters of spiritual and moral significance, these radical differences do not ignore the common ordering each creature participates in as a creature created by God, for "there is a solidarity among all creatures arising from the fact that all have the same Creator and are all ordered to his glory."[3]

The *Catechism* articulates the Thomistic principle forcefully: "Each creature possesses its own particular goodness and perfection," and that, "By the very nature of creation, material being is endowed with its own stability, truth and excellence, its own order and laws."[4] Here it affirms what we've tried to express in previous chapters: that the world that surrounds us discloses a facet of the Divine. Nature is norm in this ethical milieu, because it frames the basis for the ethical evaluation of the treatment of creatures, including each other. Because each of us participates in the Divine presence, "Man must therefore respect the particular goodness of every creature, to avoid any disordered use of things which would be in contempt of the Creator and would bring disastrous consequences for human beings and their environment."[5]

Matthew Scully, in his defense of the dignity and ethical treatment of animals, captures well the normative dimension of creatures and their natures when he says,

> Every being has a nature, and that nature defines
> the needs and ultimate good for which it exists. In

[3] CCC 334.
[4] CCC 339, referencing GS, 36.1.
[5] CCC 339.

discerning these purposes we perceive what that being is, what it can do, what it must do to find its completion and fulfillment, and therefore what its moral interests are and how they may be advanced or hindered.[6]

The livelihood of creatures, "interested" or otherwise, reflects the Divine Providence at work throughout the universe, and their preservation in the ordering of this splendid earth a participation in the exercise of His governance. Note, too, Scully's transition from the being of the creature to its ethical milieu. Integral ecology, like all natural law applications, rejects the now common division between factual claims and ethical evaluation. The flourishing of the creature points to its interests, and its existence as depending upon God establishes its valuation. Facts are distinct from ethical analyses in the conceptual order, but are united in reality, for the factual "world" to which we refer is objectively thick with intrinsic meaning and goodness. To the extent we are beholden to the God who calls the creatures forth, we are beholden to an ethically suitable manner of their treatment. "Suddenly," Scully continues, "all is not arbitrary and we have a fixed point of reference, an intelligent basis for calling one thing good and another bad. That which advances a being onward toward its natural fulfillment is good. That which frustrates or perverts its natural development is bad."[7]

---

[6] Matthew Scully, *Dominion: The Power of Man, the Suffering of Animals, and the Call to Mercy* (New York: St. Martin's Press, 2002), 300.
[7] Ibid.

Honing one's ethical sensitivity to consider the plight of animals and their treatment, especially within the industrial food systems, seems only a natural extension of an integrating ecology and builds upon the insights and foundations well established in the theological tradition. Pope Francis confirms that attitudes toward the protection of creation impact attitudes towards the protection of human life. It seems long overdue, then, that the two ideologies which are often poised against each other (pro-life vs. pro-animal) in the culture wars could find common cause in ethical concerns. Respect for creatures at large ought to lead to respect for creatures in the womb.

Does the recognition of the livelihood of creatures and the ethical demands they place upon us extend to the plant and organic orders as well? From the perspective of integral ecology, there is no reason to exclude them. It no doubt entails a greater moral imagination to consider the flourishing of insects and the like, but as creatures who are also willed into being by God, they ought not escape moral consideration, and this not only for their essential benefits to the human community, but for their intrinsic value as creatures.

The volatile debates surrounding the ethics of GMOs (genetically modified organisms) raise much deeper levels of consideration and concern, especially in light of their wide scale use and adoption by farmers here in the United States. Significant pressures are also brought upon foreign countries to adopt such biotechnologies. Many have recognized that the application of this technology comes embedded in economic systems which include elaborate infrastructures and financial support, including large scale food processes and readily available fossil fuel supplies. As such, less developed countries are caught in a web of economic circumstances which undermine their authentic human flourishing despite the promise of these technologies.

But beyond the economic and utilitarian criticisms one might bring to bear on the adoption of GMO technology, are there other values to be brought into analysis and consideration?

Remembering the bold claims of the *Catechism*: nothing exists that does not owe its existence to God the Creator (338); each creature possesses its own particular goodness (339); God wills the interdependence of each creature (340); and, finally, the beauty of creation reflects the infinite beauty of the Creator and ought to inspire the respect and submission of man's intellect and will (341); the concerns raised by critics of genetic modification will need to be fully assessed in light of this vital moral vision.

For it follows that if it is we who are darkened by sin and the creature is not, a certain deference to its intelligibility would be the only prudent measure to take. The precautionary principle of Catholic social thought applies most forcefully in the treatment of lower creation, because it is our ways, not the creatures' ways, which are caught up in the drama of sin. Recovering the philosophical tradition which takes creation seriously is the surest way to enrich an understanding of how creation's art is to be grasped and thus prudently used for the benefit of all and the glory of God. For the world points toward a rationality that transcends brute matter; the principles of form (coherence) and finality (purpose) illuminate a divine benevolence at work in the order and beauty of the world. The gift of creation that surrounds us, moreover, exceeds the comprehension of any human intelligence. Speaking of the importance of faith and 'believing in the evidence of things not seen,' Thomas poignantly remarks that "our manner of knowing is so weak that no philosopher could perfectly investigate the nature of even one little fly."[8]

Doesn't it follow that before we propose to modify nature to suit expectations, it would be wise to consider how our own ways of acting may be in need of modification? Before we ignore the coherence and purpose of living things—the distinctive principles of organic life—we might pause to consider how our biases lend themselves to reducing the created world to mere artifacts, and thus the task of stewardship to mere industry. The deliberate, transgenetic modification of a naturally occurring creature is not just an exercise in human ingenuity; it is a recasting of the creature as a mere product of human making. If unchecked by the norms of prudence, such practices run the risk of deforming creation, whose original wisdom is our norm, of transforming the creature into a "resource" whose value is merely to be "used." It is not a question of using creatures for the benefit of humankind and the glory of God. It is rather a question of the norms for such use, norms which are not only written in the human heart, but written into creation itself from the beginning.[9]

[8] Thomas Aquinas, *The Sermon-Conferences of St. Thomas Aquinas on The Apostles Creed*, trans. and ed. Nicholas Ayo, CSC. (Notre Dame: University of Notre Dame Press, 1988), 21.

[9] *Compendium of the Social Doctrine of the Church*, nos. 458–459.

When our use of creation involves the manipulation of its very structures and natural purposes, as in the case of the transgenetic modification of creatures, such an enterprise cannot be undertaken except in deliberate deference to the order and wisdom of creation of which the creature is a part: with utmost care and prudent circumspection, when proportionate goods are clearly identified and reasonably expected, and all other reasonable alternatives have been considered, including the modification of one's lifestyle.

Laudato si' puts the matter forcefully when it says, "If objective information suggests that serious and irreversible damage may result, a project should be halted or modified, even in the absence of indisputable proof. Here the burden of proof is effectively reversed, since in such cases objective and conclusive demonstrations will have to be brought forward to demonstrate that the proposed activity will not cause serious harm to the environment or to those who inhabit it."[10] Because each creature is granted a certain kind of standing within creation, a proportionate good would have to be articulated before one proceeded to modify the circumstances of any creature's well-being. It is not a matter of implementing risk assessment protocols alone, which tend to focus on outcomes and consequences, but of making a prior commitment to creatures-as-given—a preferential option for creatures—as thus having positive worth in the overall valuation.[11] Even if no significant impact is anticipated in light of one's proposed action, there remains the positive obliga-

---

[10] *LS,* no. 186.
[11] See The Cartagena Protocol at https://bch.cbd.int/ protocol.

tion to consider whether any action ought to be undertaken in the first place. What is the proportionate good intended to be achieved? Are there other, non-interventionist, natural ways of achieving similar outcomes? Can such outcomes be achieved through a more equitable distribution of goods and resources socially, for example, or is the "proportionate good" merely the perpetuation of disordered consumption on the part of the few?

Swatting a mosquito might seem innocent enough and for the sake of a pleasant evening among friends, a proportionate good is legitimately pursued in the use of bug spray. But an unmitigated hatred of any intrusive pest, exterminated to the utmost through the theatre of full-scale chemical warfare, can exceed the limits of prudence and due regard and needs to be evaluated and curtailed in light of commitments to creation and its Creator. The Four Pests Campaign of Chairman Mao Tse Tung and his communist regime is enough of a reminder that decisions about seemingly inconsequential creatures can have a devastating impact on the broader community.

Suppose for his sixtieth birthday a man were to decide to purchase a piece of forest simply for the sake of burning it down. He likes fires and experiences a kind of adrenaline rush that comes from the roar of the open flames. I believe many would see this as an exercise of intemperance and our convictions about creatures and their standing would apply in this case. The objection is not that this particular tree or this particular shrub bears any particular significance (presuming they are not an endangered species); rather, it is the fact that their destruction serves no other aim than the passing entertainment of a fragile ego. A proportionate good must be reasonably expected. This case fails the test.

The examples could be multiplied *ad nauseam* and illustrate the same point: that the willful destruction of any creature warrants an account of the proportionate good to be achieved in one's actions. Creatures are not the mere stuff of my unbridled manipulation, but are the gifts of the Creator for the sake of the common good; and to esteem them in a light any lesser than their status deserves is to demean the Creator from which they come.[12] There is a hierarchy of values at work in the world, with the human person occupying the highest rank among the embodied creatures of the earth. And while many in the environmental movement deeply resent any language of hierarchy, its absence deracinates any chance of a hierarchy of obligations which thereby follow from it. To place humans at the top of the value chain may appear excessively androcentric, but it also places the burden of ethical responsibility squarely where it belongs. Capacity makes for responsibility. The hierarchy does not give carte blanche, but instead calls out the very need for an accounting of one's actions. We must make a reasonable defense of actions in light of an ordering of creation that obliges us. While many in the Catholic tradition are familiar with such hierarchical claims at the more general and universal levels of abstraction, far too few are willing to translate these values "downward" into the particular circumstances of other living creatures and defend the standing of such creatures and their habitats. The thoughts of Czech philosopher Erazim Kohák come to mind:

[12] *SCG* III 69.

When we conceive of the world as God's creation, we cannot dismiss even the boulder as "dead matter" in our modern sense. Even the boulder is an expression of God's loving will, testifying to the glory of its maker—and as such, to be approached with respect. Its relation to us is personal in the sense that it, too, is part of a value-endowed, meaningfully oriented cosmos. In such a cosmos, the human, whether in his knowing, his feeling, or his willing, cannot proceed as a sovereign master of a meaningless reserve of raw materials. His being in the world is ordered by a moral law. He owes his world respect as a dweller therein. In turn, in such a world he is never an alien, never a stranger. His being, too, as well as his conception of it, are basically personal and personalistic.[13]

Kohák's insight, coupled with a broader Thomistic framework, forms the outline of a sustained and warranted critique of those who deface, for example, ancient rock formations in our national parks and settings. The infamous episode of scouts (who are trained to know better) toppling unique rock formations in Utah's Goblin National Park raised the need to articulate more clearly the responsibilities to each other in the care and keep of our common home—even when it comes to things as simple as rock formations.

---

[13] Erazim Kohák, *The Embers and the Stars: A Philosophical Inquiry into the Moral Sense of Nature* (Chicago: The University of Chicago Press, 1984), 210.

Theories of evolutionary development do not render null a philosophical commitment to the form and finality of creatures, for while the evidence supports the development of varying capacities over millennia, their *present* coherence and collaboration is enough to warrant ethical regard. Ecology demands a commitment to a universe in which being and goodness are convertible, in which the existence of things (even as they may evolve in their manner of being) is valued as an intrinsic good to behold and respect. It rejects the facile notion that, "All we can understand from 'nature is the naked facticity of a reality; ... nothing else."[14] St. Thomas gives to the Christian West one of the most substantive defenses of such a worldview. Green Thomists seek to renew it.[15]

At the same time, the appeal to proportionate goods points to the importance of prudence and precludes the notion that the deliberate modification of lower creation is intrinsically disordered. Nonetheless, prudence would demand the greatest circumspection, especially in the case of GMOs and related technologies. Because "we are not yet in a position to assess the biological disturbance that could result from indiscriminate genetic manipulation and from the unscrupulous development of new forms of plant and animal life, to say nothing of unacceptable ex-

---

[14] Todd A. Salzman and Michael G. Lawler, *The Sexual Person: Toward a Renewed Catholic Anthropology* (Washington, D.C.: Georgetown University Press, 2008) 49.

[15] See the work of Nicanor Austriaco, O.P., James Brent, O.P., Thomas Davenport, O.P., and Jean Baptist Ku, O.P., *Thomistic Evolution: A Catholic Approach to Understanding Evolution in the Light of Faith* (Tacoma, WA: Cluny Media, 2016).

perimentation regarding the origins of human life itself," it is only wise to counsel against such practices.[16]

As the International Theological Commission so ably expresses:

> Science and technology must be put in the service of the divine design for the whole of creation and for all creatures. This design gives meaning to the universe and to human enterprise as well. Human stewardship of the created world is precisely a stewardship exercised by way of participation in the divine rule and is always subject to it. Human beings exercise this stewardship by gaining scientific understanding of the universe, by caring responsibly for the natural world (including animals and the environment) and by guarding their own biological integrity.[17]

It is not a question of using creatures for the benefit of all and the glory of God. It is rather a question of the norms for such use, norms which are not only discerned in the human heart but written into creation itself from the beginning.[18] The authentic exercise of prudence would require a host of allied virtues, including temperance, jus-

---

[16] *Compendium of the Social Doctrine of the Church*, 459.

[17] International Theological Commission, *Communion and Stewardship: Human Persons Created in the Image of God*, (2002), no. 61, at http://www.vatican.va/roman_curia/congregations/cfaith/cti_documents/rc_con_cfaith_doc_20040723_communion-stewardship_en.html.

[18] *Compendium of the Social Doctrine of the Church*, 458–459. For a broader discussion see, *Vocation of the Agricultural Leader* (Vatican City: International Catholic Rural Association, 2016).

tice, and fortitude. Strengthened by the light of faith, these infused qualities of character can only further enable the Catholic faithful to take up the questions of stewardship and articulate a robust vision of environmental care.

* * * * *

For St. Thomas the cosmos was created, sustained, governed, divinely appointed, and ordered to manifest the glory of God. We, too, are no exception to this general rule of Divine munificence. Our vocation as embodied spiritual creatures is to come to know and love this God, partially in this life as Creator and Redeemer, completely in the next as mutually indwelling friend.

The Eternal law identifies the governing providence of the entire order of things; the natural law, our unique participation in that ordering. The principal enactment of the natural law is through the exercise of sound reasoning and ordered willing, but it is always the reasoning of a creature of the earth. And thus the natural law, by the nature of its very exercise, extends to the realms of the embodied order of things. Biological processes are never irrelevant for those creatures who are tasked with the enactment of the Eternal law as a community of creatures yoked to the earth. We are to live *secundam naturam*, in accord with the dignity of embodied, created natures.

When St. Thomas seeks to fill in the various precepts of a natural law ethic, he appeals to the notion of the human person as reflecting the kind of ordered activity one sees throughout the various levels of creation. He observes that all creatures seek to sustain themselves and avoid obstacles that prohibit their growth and development, and thus protecting human life and health is a feature of the natural law. He sees that animals, in particular, seek to propagate their kind, and thus it is suitable that human beings seek the same in a manner consistent with their own unique dignity. Finally, he affirms our unique character as creatures endowed with intellect and will, and so it is that the natural law affirms a natural inclination to know the truth about God, to shun ignorance, and to live in ordered community.

Because in man there is first of all an inclination to good in accordance with the nature which he has in common with all substances: inasmuch as every substance seeks the preservation of its own being, according to its nature: and by reason of this inclination, whatever is a means of preserving human life, and of warding off its obstacles, belongs to the natural law. Secondly, there is in man an inclination to things that pertain to him more specially, according to that nature which he has in common with other animals: and in virtue of this inclination, those things are said to belong to the natural law, "which nature has taught to all animals," such as sexual intercourse, the education of offspring and so forth. Thirdly, there is in man an inclination to good, according to the nature of his reason which nature is proper to him: thus man has a natural inclination to know the truth about God, and to live in society: and in this respect, whatever pertains to this inclination belongs to the natural law; for instance, to shun ignorance, to avoid offending those among whom one has to live, and other such things regarding the above inclination.[19]

Note that the overall account of the natural law is not derived from some speculative meditation on the principles of human dignity or some highly conceptualized analysis of the nature of reason itself. Rather, St. Thomas turns to the ordering one finds in nature to provide the basic outlines of natural law. Creation and its creatures as given in ordinary experience provide the benchmarks for appropriate behavior and its demands. Nature discloses the outlines of a norm in both Catholic and organic circles, and the order among creatures both human and organic alike have a value and compelling standing, if you will, in moral analysis.

Integral ecology is consistent with this conviction, for it, too, sees the human person within the broader framework of an ethically rich order of living beings and calls forth all of those who are willing to recognize a wisdom in the natural order of things. Here lies an important opportunity to unite in common cause the defenders of creatures and the aspirations of many Catholic Christians. And it is time for us to think boldly and courageously as Pope Francis has asked.

The respect that is called out in deference to the organic systems of the plant and animal orders equally applies to our own bodies as well. Thomas rejects the notion that we are organisms attached to plants which are attached to an intellect and will, and so he rejects the theory of "multiple souls" or multiple principles of guiding

---

[19] *ST* I-II. 94.2.

activities within the human person. Instead, he recognizes a hierarchy of participated being, and sees in the human person what is replicated in the animal and plant orders. We are spiritual beings and not merely animals, but we reflect our animality through the exercise of our sensitive powers; we are not plants, but we reflect those organic processes in our bodies through what Thomas calls "vegetative powers." Just as the order of plants and animals was not impacted by sin, so too, the sensitive and vegetative operations of the human person remain normative—assuming they are functioning in a healthy way and not interfered with by disordered thinking or choices.

It is precisely this confidence in organic processes generally that establishes the foundations for the Church's teachings on many of the issues concerning the right "use" of one's body in particular. Because the body in its organic activity reflects the divine wisdom at work, the body provides the outlines of a normative order of behavior. To deliberately intend to destroy the organic operations of the human person is to act "*contra naturam*" and signals a serious assault on the dignity of the human person. Thus to poison, mutilate, or cause physical harm or serious illness to another human being is contrary to their dignity and is never morally permissible. Our sensitive powers, too, demand respect. And thus to deliberately mutilate, deform, or otherwise damage the body is considered immoral. The deliberate intention to render one's otherwise fertile intercourse infertile, either temporarily or permanently, is considered an attack on the embodied character of the human person and is thus prohibited in the Catholic moral tradition.

Notice how important the "biological" dimensions of the human person are here in determining at least the negative norm: those activities which ought never to be done. This is not a mere "physicalism" because we recognize that the discussion here doesn't capture everything about the moral life governing the "use" of the body. We have not (nor will we in this chapter), for example, discussed the status of the person as having an intellect and will, and thus being capable of love, respect, and commitment (also essential for normative human relationships). For the same reason, to recognize the organic character of human living is not to fall prey to the standard criticism that "biology is destiny." If the argument were that *only* the organic processes of the human person were the sum total of the moral norm, then the accusations of a brutish physicalism would be fair. Instead something different is asserted here: while the human person is never exhausted by the categories of organic activity, they neither escape the ordering of that activity. And it is the systemic resentment of the organic order of things, the glorious world of the body and its stuff, that has created the toxic climate that surrounds contemporary culture, including Catholic culture.

Green Thomists refuse to concede to neo-Manichaean monopolists the dignity of the person as an organic being, as a creature of the earth, among the earth and its creatures. Indeed, were it not for the graciousness of God, who leaves a vestige of His divine wisdom in the first book of the world, including the body, we would be marooned on the loneliest of spaces, adrift in a world void of meaning, starved for truth.

The defense of the organic ordering of things, whether in the human body or other bodies, provides the extraordinary occasion to unite in common cause and mutual understanding various groups of sincere individuals who are so often opposed: those who promote organic practices in the garden bed, those who promote organic practices in the marriage bed. Green Thomism works for the day when the joyful discovery of the divine wisdom in all of God's bodies can be uniformly celebrated in every facet of living. Pope Francis calls for a bold new thinking. It is time to form bold new communities of thought. The invitation must go both ways.

Why not include natural family planning as a program in integral ecology? Why not consider national parks as the newest mission territory so apt for evangelization? Why isn't the organic food movement, or the animal rights movement, and the celebration of life it so often represents, united in common cause with the defense of human life? "In creation," the Church tells us, "God laid a foundation and established laws that remain firm, on which the believer can rely with confidence, for they are the sign and pledge of the unshakeable faithfulness of God's covenant. For his part man must remain faithful to this foundation, and respect the laws which the Creator has written into it."[20] For so many people in the journey of faith, the beauty of creation is their first tutor, the first experience of the presence of the divine in a compelling and important way. We need to build upon that experience in whatever manner it may come

[20] CCC 346.

about, whether in discovering the wisdom of fertility in the well-tended fields or the wisdom of fertility in the life of the chaste couple.

Someday a cadre of permanent deacons and their families, attuned to the thought of St. Thomas and the beauty of creation, will commit a portion of their summers to serving the pastoral needs of the millions of itinerant seekers who turn to the world of wilderness in search of a modern sanctuary. Diocesan priests will be introduced to these challenges in their preparation for priesthood. They, unlike the religious, seem especially blessed for such a task, for in committing to a diocese, they permanently pledge themselves to a place, a parcel of earth, and to promote the Gospel to whomever crosses their path. A diocesan vocation is uniquely situated among the priestly apostolates, for the priest commits himself to a region and locale, to his bishop "and his successors," signaling a fundamental promise of stability to a region. Their institutions could guide their local communities in a manner unsurpassed toward ecological integrity, for they would have the advantage of a long-range commitment, something so crucially lacking in today's itinerant peoples.

And lay professionals everywhere will enter the cause especially and in their expertise develop a new kind of ecological casuistry in which the creature is granted standing in order to guide consciences in matters of the prudential use of things. Practicing integral ecology will demand a habit of mind which takes into consideration that to determine whether an action is permissible, "we must look not to the action alone, but to the action in its total context," a context that now includes the impact of one's decisions on the environment.[21]

* * * * *

The lower orders of creatures were untouched, we have said, as well as those capacities in our own souls which we imitate with other ranks of being: with the plants, a desire for health and growth; with the animals, a desire to procreate.[22] These remain intact to the extent they are not disturbed "from above," as it were, by a disordered reason and a weakened will—which bends my natural desire for health into gluttony, my natural desire for development into avarice, and my natural desire for family into lust. It can be a sobering occasion of deep-seated humility to discover in one's self the extent to which a life that is *contra naturam* has taken over one's world of experience—until one steps out in faith.

And so faith is offered to those who sincerely ask, found by those who truly seek, opened to those who humbly knock. The grace of Christ, inaugurated in Baptism, sends a healing balm through the secret of one's soul, warming the intellect by His truth and softening the will by His love. Though it is never fully completed in this life, holiness thus becomes the privileged task we now humbly yet confidently undertake as the newly adopted son or daughter of the Owner of this splendid universe spread before us. The natural law which still binds us to the role as a "tiller and keeper" of the earth is now infused with the new law of grace whereby He no longer sees us as mere stewards of

---

[21] Philip Keane, S.S., *Sexual Morality: A Catholic Perspective* (New York: Paulist Press, 1977), 46.

[22] Cf. *ST* I-II 98.4 ad 3; *ST* I-II 106.3 ad 3.

His household, but as friends of the God Himself. We no longer live merely in accordance with the laws of being, but in light of the love of the Creator and the glory of God.

Reason is strengthened by faith, the light we once dimly perceived in the furthest reaches of my night, now shines ever-so-faintly, yet ever more clearly. The vision of a cold abyss of a godless expanse is overthrown by the presence of an Other. Like an evening fire at one's feet, the warmth of His grace begins to infuse our being. A stiff neck is made supple, a tensed body becomes at peace, and a *quies* descends and we rest at the hearth of the Lord.

The will, too, discovers a new freedom from compulsion, a winsomeness once only observed at a jealous distance in others. The cacophony of busyness settles into the jazz of life, as we weave a soulful tune through the accompaniment of communion—with the world, with others, with God. Strengthened in truth, we can walk with greater confidence, not the timid tiptoe of a fragile, frightened ego. Of course there is failure, given the cloud of woundedness, but the shadows are now a mere counterpoint, a confirmation that we walk in the light.

It was the inescapable beauty of the cosmos that led Paul to condemn those who were blinded to the reality of God as "without excuse" (see Rom 1:20); as such they allowed the darkness of sin to usurp the originative ordering of their dreams and desires. The same power of the beauty of things leads Thomas down the path discerning the reasonableness of our natural inclinations as well as the claim that God became Incarnate in Jesus Christ (see Jn 20:24–29). Through it all lies a confidence in *natura*, the panoply of divine light refracted freely about the universe that mirrors the Wisdom of the Divine to this day. Now suffering from a spiritual glaucoma at our origins, we have to feel our way through the things of the universe, never far from stumbling, ever in need of the healing grace of Jesus Christ. As the latest sons and daughters adopted by the Father, in Christ, the task at the center of integral ecology can now be made complete, for in Him we have been given the answer to the question that confronts us at the crimson dawn of each day, under the diamond dome of each night: how can we make a return to the Lord, for all that He has bestowed on us?

SELECTED READINGS FOR CHAPTER SEVEN

On Whether the Multitude and Distinction of Things Come from God?

We must say that the distinction and multitude of things come from the intention of the first agent, who is God. For He brought things into being in order that His goodness might be communicated to creatures, and be represented by them; and because His goodness could not be adequately represented by one creature alone, He produced many and diverse creatures, that what was wanting to one in the representation of the divine goodness might be supplied by another. For goodness, which in God is simple and uniform, in creatures is manifold and divided and hence the whole universe together participates in the divine goodness more perfectly, and represents it better than any single creature whatever.

—St. Thomas Aquinas, *ST* I 47.1

On Living Fully the Dimensions of Conversion

Various convictions of our faith, developed at the beginning of this Encyclical can help us to enrich the meaning of this conversion. These include the awareness that each creature reflects something of God and has a message to convey to us, and the security that Christ has taken unto Himself this material world and now, risen, is intimately present to each being, surrounding it with his affection and penetrating it with his light. Then too, there is the recognition that God created the world, writing into it an order and a dynamism that human beings have no right to ignore. We read in the Gospel that Jesus says of the birds of the air that "not one of them is forgotten before God" (Lk 12:6). How then can we possibly mistreat them or cause them harm? I ask all Christians to recognize and to live fully this dimension of their conversion. May the power and the light of the grace we have received also be evident in our relationship to other creatures and to the world around us. In this way, we will help nurture that sublime fraternity with all creation which St. Francis of Assisi so radiantly embodied.

—Pope Francis, *LS*, no. 221

The Dignity of the Land and the Body

Two groups, object to modern technologies, appealing to natural law, offer alternatives that, through cooperation with nature, promote health and community—and yet they are typically considered opponents. This perceived division stems largely from a notion that is very commonly held, unfortunately even by many Catholics and organic advocates, although it stands against their over-all philosophies; the notion that there is a kind of moral barrier between the human body and the rest of creation, the idea that the "nature" of the body and the "nature" of the land are so radically different that they call for entire-ly divergent kinds of moral concern. Too often this type of thinking affects those who otherwise stand for natural law. The NFP advocate is passionate about maintaining a cooperative relationship to the nature of her body, but has little interest in the natural sources of that body's food, and may even seek to undermine the natural systems of her garden with Round-up and Miracle Gro. The organic farmer takes pains to preserve the natural fertility of the soil, but his own body's fertility he deposits in latex and sends to the landfill. They agree that the body and the land are somehow isolated; to the one they grant all the care and respect demanded by natural law, while the other they relegate to thoughtless use.

But the perspective of the natural law does not sup-port this view; the connections between the body and the land are real and unavoidable. Our ancestors were aware of these connections and enshrined them in language, in those words that still bind together sex and agriculture: seed, fertility, fruit, husbandry. "No matter how urban our life," says Wendell Berry in *The Unsettling of America* (1986), "our bodies live by farming; we came from the earth and return to it, and so we live in agriculture as we live in flesh." Likewise, the *Catechism of the Catholic Church* affirms that in sexuality, "man's belonging to the bodily and biological world is expressed" (2337). We are bound to the land and to one another by the reproduction of farming and the reproduction of sex, and it ought not surprise us, as Berry puts it, that "there should be some profound resemblance between our treatment of our bodies and our treatment of the earth." The industrial mind that has given us "birth control" has also given us "pest control." The way of healing, connection and responsibility can be discovered only by the mind informed by natural law, the mind that, as Berry says, "prefers the Creation itself to the powers and quantities to which it can be reduced."

—Christopher Killheffer, "Organic Sex, Organic Farming,"
Pilgrim: A Journal of Catholic Experience (Lent/Easter 2011),
at http://www.pilgrimjournal.com/organic_sex.html

SELECTED RESOURCES FOR CHAPTER SEVEN

Joseph Pearce, *Small is Still Beautiful: Economics as if Families Mattered* (Wilmington, DE: ISI Books, 2006).

Wendell Berry, "Two Economies," in *Home Economics* (New York, NY: North Point Press, 1987), 54–75.

Christopher Franks, *He Became Poor: The Poverty of Christ and Aquinas's Economic Teachings* (Grand Rapids, MI: Eerdmans, 2009).

·❊·

CHAPTER EIGHT

THE IMPULSE TO GRATITUDE

"It would scarcely accord with the character of divine goodness were God to keep his knowledge to Himself without intimately disclosing Himself to others, since to be generous is of the nature of the good."[1]

THE Kawuneeche Valley spreads out before me, a once verdant meadow turned straw in this fall season of the year. And again, a Lapis Lazuli vault spans the valley, this time dusted with the faintest suggestions of clouds along the eastern rise. Aspen tapers glow and throw a honey-lustre over the bluegreen tapestries of fir, pine, and spruce. Over the wash of Colorado, a bull-elk intones his approval, an antiphon in the hymnody of life: his universal, urgent cry for communion: "Make a joyful noise to the Lord, all the lands! Serve the Lord with gladness! Come into his presence with singing!" (Ps 100:1–2). Once again, as with every dawn, the Invitatory begins

---

[1] *Opusc.* XIV, *Exposition, de divinis nominibus*, i, *lect* I, in Gilby, 32.

amidst the stirring of things. They know no fault, no lingering nostalgia; nothing in their timing suggests a "then" or a "now." There is no golden age in creation, nor anxious anticipation of an eschaton. Creatures dwell in the house of the Lord wherein one day is as a thousand years.

And I, too, in this temple of creation feel the chorus of life swell within my being and rise in response. What Jean-Louis Chrétien calls "the shock of beauty" calls out nothing less than a "yes" on my part. And so I rise to my feet, lift my eyes, and with hands raised, I pray. These bonds of being drag me out of my self-slumber into the joyful wakefulness of praise. Beauty dilates the soul, permits it to be moved by an other, disposes it to the presence of an other, and creates the setting for epiphany. It makes us vulnerable to the true and the good, and teaches us what Thomas means when he says that love can take up where knowledge ends.[2]

There is a law of exigency, an irresistible impulse, which wells up from within when in the presence of beauty. It calls forth a response of some kind, of gratitude and return, of remembrance and reform, an unfinished task, to wonder with the Psalmist: "What shall I render to the Lord for all his bounty to me? I will lift up the cup of salvation and call on the name of the Lord" (Ps 116:12–13).

Stir the embers once again and let prayer wend its way among the stars. Pause in silence above the glen "and let the soft animal of your body love what it loves."[3] I

[2] *ST* II-II 27.4 ad 1.
[3] Mary Oliver, "Wild Geese," in *Dream Work* (New York: Atlantic Monthly Press, 1986), 14.

can not begrudge any who have felt, however vaguely, the deep-seated need to praise the One through whom all good things come. I feel empathy for Coleridge and his modern companions who journey through the vistas of our national parks, in pilgrimage to that One they ardently love and urgently seek.

> So will I build my altar in the fields,
> And the blue sky my fretted dome shall be,
> And the sweet fragrance that the wild flower
>   yields
> Shall be the incense I will yield to Thee,
> Thee only God! and thou shalt not despise
> Even me, the priest of this poor sacrifice.[4]

* * * * *

I have empathy for those who seek the Logos, perhaps unwittingly, because the Logos waited patiently for me. At the service of humanity, the Church, too, walks in pilgrimage, in accompaniment with all of those who, in discovering the beauty of nature, discern the presence of the Divine. And so with them and all the creatures we blend voices with this valley's Lauds:

> The heavens are telling the glory of God;
>   and the firmament proclaims his handiwork.
> Day to day pours forth speech,
>   and night to night declares knowledge.

---

4   Samuel Taylor Coleridge, "To Nature," in *Samuel Taylor Coleridge, The Complete Poems*, ed. William Keach (London: Penguin Classics, 1997), 370.

There is no speech, nor are there words;
 their voice is not heard;
yet their voice goes out through all the earth,
 and their words to the end of the world.
  (Ps 19:1–4)

They have no speech, nor are there words. But I speak, and my voice is heard—or is it? I sing my "Amen" in the woods of the world. Is it heard? That is the thing: to feel grateful for "all this "juice and all this joy," yet wonder whether it is enough.[5] I do not want to merely feel grateful. I want to be grateful, and being grateful, as opposed to merely feeling grateful, requires at least two conditions: that I recognize myself as one having received; and that I be recognized by the Other as grateful.

Beauty is not arrived at through some discursive process; it is not something I achieve through personal effort or determination. Coming upon the unexpected seems to be a condition of the encounter with beauty; otherwise, I would conjure beauty in my imagination on my own terms and my own willing. But the beautiful, especially in nature, is not of my own making. It is something given to me from outside of myself. Like grace, its origins lie in the generosity of the Other to grant to me the experience of the beautiful. My task—even if that is too strong a word—is to be disposed to it, to allow myself to be vulnerable to its in-break. Beauty is the voice of creation that

---

[5] Gerard Manley Hopkins, "Spring," in *Gerard Manley Hopkins, Poems and Prose*, ed. W. H. Gardner (London: Penguin Classics, 1985), 28.

makes way for the Word. Because beauty both illumines the condition of my receptivity as well as the impulse to respond, it is among the closest of natural analogues to the presence of God's grace in our lives.

Gratitude, from *gratis*, is the response of someone who has received a gift—a gift from another. One cannot be grateful and at the same time be alone. Gratitude before creation is a deeply personal affair, but it cannot be a solitary one. If I am to fulfill the urge to gratitude that wells up spontaneously within me in the face of this gift of a universe, I need an other, the Other, as the proper object of my gratitude.

"Object" is not quite the right word. For one can only be grateful to an Other who is giving, giving in freedom of course—the freedom of Someone, not something. And so the immense feeling of gratitude before the splendor of things places one immediately in a relationship to an Other who is free, generous, capable of giving gifts, personal. The grateful joy that is released from the deepest recesses of ourselves in the presence of the beautiful is the experiential, though unthematic, affirmation of the invisible God.

Gratitude, St. Thomas says, impels us to give back more than has been received and in the same generosity of spirit with which it has been given.[6] While natural in its movement, it is no longer spontaneously achieved. Sin clots the source, redirects one's attention to immediate concerns, stiffens the neck so as to miss the vista, preoccupies the mind with anxious distraction. Sin distorts the

---

[6] *ST* II-II 106.6.

message, takes the innocent moment and smears it with the darkest of motives in wish-fulfillment, authority complexes, ontic anxieties, and the rest. Sin steals the Sabbath, the contemplative resting in the garden of being, turns the mind to ardor and achievement, duty and destiny. Refusal is always a possibility once the earth is seen as all toil and task. The tragedy of atheism means that one can never walk gratefully "in the evening breeze."

Companions, fellow hikers, and seekers on the way, all those who patiently waited at the summit, tolerated senseless inquiries, lent a steady hand, or pointed the better route, all those in baubles and beads, braids and bandanas, the tawny and trim, the fit and the fortified, who sat around the glowing fire into the wee night hours, huddled like pilgrims in the inn of common cause, to all those peopling the parks and paths in the quest of the deeper things, I offer my gift and say: I see how humble you are, how earnestly you pursue the true, the good, and the beautiful. I see the tenderness shown to neighbors great and small and the wonder you pay freely to the many creatures around you. You model a life of simplicity and gratitude and your earnest search is an edifying testimony to your integrity. But I, a fellow pilgrim in the company of gratitude, suggest that the end of the search points to a Person and not a place, a Someone and not a something. That our gratitude is not in the least misplaced, but is unfilled if not united to that One from whom all good gifts come. "Ever since the creation of the world his invisible nature, namely, his eternal power and deity, has been clearly perceived in the things that have been made" (Rom 1:20).

Grateful joy bids us forth. We would betray the quest, if having discovered the summit, not taken the courage to finally ascend. All of the sacrifice, the ardor and effort, the patience and plodding, the aches and pains, pitfalls and problems, all come to a moment of decision: to follow the path to its end . . . or to refuse it. We are, after all, sons of Adam and daughters of Eve, sadly under the spell of the Fall. In which case, in refusing gratitude, we come to see that we are not so much hiking as hiding. We are not so much on a journey of discovery as engaged in a strategy not to be discovered. We do not take time to "get away" as much as we hope all of life would "go away." We delight in creatures, having dread of the Creator. Under the shadow, we cannot discover gratitude with the ease we might have once had.

But if we choose the path of gratitude, then let's follow it fully—gratefully. We cannot help but be grateful to the One who has shared all of these things. This One is the veiled presence of the Logos of which the ancient witnesses speak, the *Kalon* of the Greeks, Yahweh of ancient Israel, the One who has now taken flesh in the person of Jesus Christ. As the Prologue of John so eloquently puts it:

In the beginning was the Word, and the Word was with God, and the Word was God. He was in the beginning with God; all things were made through him, and without him was not anything made that was made. . . . And the Word became flesh and dwelt among us, full of grace and truth; we have beheld his glory, glory as of the only Son from the Father. (Jn 1:1–3, 14)

There on the turnout to the overlook, hovering above the tree line and huddled among the clouds, there in the evening light along the shore's easy wash of water, there in the sylvan symphony of a summer woods, Christ the Logos bids us come closer, for

> He is the image of the invisible God, the first-born of all creation; for in him all things were created, in heaven and on earth, visible and invisible, whether thrones or dominions or principalities or authorities—all things were created through him and for him. He is before all things, and in Him all things hold together. (Col 1:15–17)

This awe that we feel at the precipice of the stars, this majesty that overwhelms us at every morning's menu, this gratitude that wells up from within is not merely the outburst of a strangely emotive personality, or the misplaced sentiment of a misfit of the universe; awe is the irrepressible response of a fully alive creature of God, a spirited son or daughter caught up in the divine play of His creation. At the top of the canyon rim, on the shores of the crystal waters, before the shafts of summer rain that draw their curtain over the horizon, we pray aloud in the secret of our hearts:

> i thank You God for most this amazing
> day: for the leaping greenly spirits of trees

and a blue true dream of sky; and for everything
which is natural which is infinite which is yes[7]

And we can thank You God by name! Jesus Christ, the
Logos, the Creator, the Redeemer, the Lord!

> Because as the Apostle Paul made it abundant-
> ly clear when he said, 'For the invisible things of
> God . . . are clearly seen, being understood by the
> things that are made,' it would seem only fitting
> (*conveniens*) that by visible things of this beautiful
> earth the invisible things of God would be made
> known; for this is the purpose the whole world
> was made. And since it belongs to the essence
> of goodness to communicate itself to others . . .
> it belongs to the essence of the highest good to
> communicate itself in the highest manner to the
> creature, and this is brought about chiefly by His
> so joining created nature to Himself.[8]

And so, Thomas says here, the Incarnation of God in the
person of Jesus Christ seems "fitting"—not "necessary," or
"self-evident," or "obvious," or "demonstrable," but rather
understandable, reasonable that the invisible God whom
we encounter in gratitude before the visible things of this
splendid universe would Himself become most visible in
the Incarnation: Jesus Christ.

---

[7] E.E. Cummings, "i thank you God for most this amazing," in E.E.
Cummings, *100 Selected Poems*, ed. E.E. Cummings (New York:
Grove Press, 1954), 114.

[8] *ST* III 1.1.

The One to whom I spontaneously feel grateful amidst all of this glorious splendor of the universe *is* the One who became Incarnate in the One Christians name Jesus. In Christ, our joy may be complete. The One whom we have been beholding in the heart of things *is* the One who is beholding us in the deepest recesses of His heart.

Let the Christ be a cairn and your life mark the way, so that others who follow in their search for the truth may discover in you the way, the truth, the life (see Jn 14:6). This is the hope of every Green Thomist, this is the goal of integral ecology: to welcome into the family of Christ all of those pilgrims of creation who may not have known the One by name, but who nonetheless calls each of them by name. We need them, all passionate lovers of the earth, we need them desperately, to complete what is lacking in the body of Christ, for the cause of integral ecology, like a spring of living water, flows beyond the edges of the familiar in every direction.

Indoor Christians could stand for renewal as well. Those who profess the truth of Christ, yet confine Him in rubric and regiment alone, can forget, and even hold in disdain, the first text and sacrament writ large all around us. *Sursum corda!* Nature belongs to Christ: in its origins through creation, in its consummation through redemption! The light we protect so tenderly in a bushel basket spirituality is better seen amidst the lampstands of the universe. The light of Christ illumines every dulled intellect and is refracted from every facet of truth, goodness, and beauty wherever it be found. One can find Christ in all things, when the aptitude for vision is nurtured by faith. Whether mired in the thickets of species and spoilage, or suffering spiritual anemia and thus allergic to life, all of us need to remember and relive the central thesis of Christian culture: God is present in every nook and cranny of the universe, waiting to be discovered in truth, contemplated in love, and celebrated in faith.

The fullest life of integral ecology demands that we unite in experience what is already one in the plan of creation. I have wandered amidst the darkened catacombs on the Appian Way and strained my neck to view the clerestories of Chartres; have adored before the vault of San Clemente; and prayed within the starkness of Santa Sabina; I have marveled at the Cathedral of York and was quieted at Gethsemani in Bardstown. But I have also seen the crashing cataracts of Austrian Alps, watched a wash of diamonds tumble into the Yosemite Valley, was refreshed in the thundering spray of Victoria Falls, and admired the cobalt surface of Lake Irene on the continental divide. The generous Lord God meets us each time and each place.

Of course, before the Blessed Sacrament, in the tabernacle of God, Christ is present in a manner unsurpassed. But the Christ is present here, too, in the tabernacle of creation. And the task of integral ecology is to love Him fiercely wherever He may be, which is wherever you are. The best place to pray is wherever prayer is best prayed. This is not to slight the cathedrals, but to see them as the eruption of the spirit from the depths of the earth. Like a great mountain surging above the tectonic plates of immense energy that surrounds it, the cathedral erupts from the irrepressible force of the Spirit penetrating matter, the Spirit in soil, the Spirit alive amidst saints yoked to the earth.

The calendar says it is the Twenty-Eighth Sunday in Ordinary Time, but the creatures of the Never Summer Range have not taken notice. There is nothing ordinary about this morning's service. Aspen leaves drip melted mountain wax on the stones of an ancient chapel. A "Te Deum" blows through the stalwart pines in their balsam hoods and rapt attention. This morning's Lauds takes place among a cathedral of pines. And a spontaneous litany of prayer wells from within like a spring of living water—called forth by Him who thirsts, for "You are also praised by all of earth's creatures each in its own way." And while there is none to compare to what we offer in the Mass, "you still delight in such tokens of love as earth can offer." And so, Lord Jesus, grant me a spirit of holy integrity, to draw all things now fractured by my sin into the single offering of praise that groans from every corner of your splendid universe. "May heaven and earth together acclaim you as king; may the praise that is sung in heaven resound in the heart of every creature on the earth."[9]

The descent. Clouds gather just beyond the western range. An early fall shower is about to commence. Adam would have seen it coming, but in my clouded ways, I cannot see that a good drenching is about to begin. It is time to retreat to the interior of my raincoat and focus my gaze to my muddy steps below. It is a perfect occasion for a recollected saunter, a rosary of rhythmic movement of mind and matter that draws us into the rest of contem-

---

[9] Psalm Prayer for the Twenty-Eighth Sunday in Ordinary Time.

plation. Come, Lord Jesus! Come, Creator and Redeemer and fill my heart! For it is not by knowledge alone that I have come into Your presence, but by desire and love, a desire first stirred in the quiet corners of Your universe, a love first born in the vestibule of Your creation, and now is made docile to Your grace. May this delight and joy, enkindled before the vistas of Your earth, impel me into the company of Your presence.

* * * * *

The First Mystery of Creation:
The Incarnation
"And the Word became flesh and dwelt among us." —John 1:14

This famous line from the opening of the Gospel of John marks an excellent point of departure for prayer for at least two reasons: first, the earth is not alien to God, not in the least. Instead, dwelling among us, God chose to enact His plan of love and redemption on this land. Second, at a deeper level, all of creation bears the impress of the Word, the Logos, the one through whom all things are made. Awe before the beauty of creation is a kind of adoration of the Son. In this first decade, we can reflect on those occasions of awe and thank God for this presence in our lives.

The Second Mystery of Creation:
The Power of Beauty
"Consider the lilies of the field, how they grow; they neither toil nor spin; yet I tell you, even Sol-

omon in all his glory was not arrayed like one of these." —Matthew 6:28–29

In this second mystery, consider something beautiful; perhaps have a flower on hand as a spiritual aid, ponder its incredible intricacy, its delicate nature, its beauty, its fragility—and yet, its power—to produce something beautiful for God. Jesus uses this occasion of a flower to remind us not to worry. God is in charge and we can take comfort in Him. In knowing something beautiful, we know God is with us. In this second decade, we can recall a wondrous location and consider how God seeks to meet and care for us there.

The Third Mystery of Creation: The Power of Christ

"What sort of man is this, that even winds and sea obey him?" —Matthew 8:27

We need to be honest; encountering nature is not always a rosy experience. Pondering the beauty of a flower is one thing; bracing for the impending storm on the horizon another. Especially with the introduction of sin, we can count on misunderstanding nature and resenting its ways. But Christ takes the occasion of ill weather to remind the disciples of the importance of faith and that inordinate fear has no place for one who rests in the Lord. In grasping the power of nature, we can learn to trust in God. In this decade, we pray for the graces to trust in the Providence of God for all creatures.

The Fourth Mystery of Creation:
The Future of Creation

"All things were created through him and for him." —Colossians 1:16

It is not unusual when standing under a starry sky to wonder: what is all of this for? Well, it's for us, in many ways. The glory of this universe is the setting in which we live out our lives in gratitude to the Father. Christ joins us in this desire, especially in the Eucharist, and it is there, in that universal prayer of the Church, that the world is given its final purpose and direction. In this decade, we pray that we may return the gifts of creation, including our labors, to the Father.

The Fifth Mystery of Creation:
The Renewal of Creation

"Behold, I make all things new." —Revelation 21:5

What is the status of the earth and its creatures in the final judgment and the kingdom? In *Laudato si'*, Pope Francis makes the bold suggestion that "eternal life will be a shared experience of awe, in which each creature, resplendently transfigured, will take its rightful place . . . " (no. 243). Though theologians have offered various interpretations, one thing is clear: the life that we lived here on earth will be fulfilled, not dismissed. How we have loved God, neighbor, and His creatures will be a testament to our faith. In this decade, we pray for the courage and hope to live out our remaining days giving thanks to the Lord for the gift of His earth.

SELECTED READINGS FOR CHAPTER EIGHT

On the "Naturalness" and "Unnaturalness" of Death

We may have a suspicion that the separation of the soul from the body is not *per accidens* but is in accord with nature. . . . In view of these considerations we must take up the question of how this separation is according to nature, and how it is opposed to nature. We showed above that the rational soul exceeds the capacity of all corporeal matter in a measure impossible to other forms. This is demonstrated by its intellectual activity, which it exercises without the body. To the end that corporeal matter might be fittingly adapted to the soul, there had to be added to the body some disposition that would make it suitable matter for such a form. And in the same way that this form itself receives existence from God alone through creation, that disposition, transcending as it does corporeal nature, was conferred on the human body by God alone for the purpose of preserving the body itself in a state of incorruption so that it might match the soul's perpetual existence. This disposition remained in man's body as long as man's soul cleaved to God.

But when man's soul turned from God by sin the human body deservedly lost that supernatural disposition whereby it was unrebelliously subservient to the soul. And hence man incurred the necessity of dying.

According, if we regard the nature of the body, death is natural. But if we regard the nature of the soul and the disposition with which the human body was supernaturally endowed in the beginning for the sake of the soul, death is *per accidens* and contrary to nature, inasmuch as union with the body is natural for the soul.

—St. Thomas Aquinas, *Compendium*, 152

On the Need for an Ecological Conversion

The rich heritage of Christian spirituality, the fruit of twenty centuries of personal and communal experience, has a precious contribution to make to the renewal of humanity. Here, I would like to offer Christians a few suggestions for an ecological spirituality grounded in the convictions of our faith, since the teachings of the Gospel have direct consequences for our way of thinking, feeling and living. More than in ideas or concepts as such, I am interested in how such a spirituality can motivate us to a more passionate concern for the protection of our world. A commitment this lofty cannot be sustained by doctrine alone, without a spirituality capable of inspiring us, without an "interior impulse which encourages, motivates, nourishes and gives meaning to our individual and communal activity." Admittedly, Christians have not always appropriated and developed the spiritual treasures bestowed by God upon the Church, where the life of the spirit is not dissociated from the body or from nature or from worldly realities, but lived in and with them, in communion with all that surrounds us.

"The external deserts in the world are growing, because the internal deserts have become so vast." For this reason, the ecological crisis is also a summons to profound interior conversion. It must be said that some committed and prayerful Christians, with the excuse of realism and pragmatism, tend to ridicule expressions of concern for the environment. Others are passive; they choose not to change their habits and thus become inconsistent. So what they all need is an "ecological conversion," whereby the effects of their encounter with Jesus Christ become evident in their relationship with the world around them. Living our vocation to be protectors of God's handiwork is essential to a life of virtue; it is not an optional or a secondary aspect of Christian experience.

In calling to mind the figure of Saint Francis of Assisi, we come to realize that a healthy relationship with creation is one dimension of overall personal conversion, which entails the recognition of our errors, sins, faults and failures, and leads to heartfelt repentance and desire to change. The Australian bishops spoke of the importance of such conversion for achieving reconciliation with creation: "To achieve such reconciliation, we must examine our lives and acknowledge the ways in which we have harmed God's creation through our actions and our failure to act. We need to experience a conversion, or change of heart."

—Pope Francis, *LS*, nos. 216–218

On Peas

"Now surely," [he said], "you cannot imagine that all these similar characters are mere coincidences. Do they not rather go to show that the Creator in making the pea vine and Locust tree had the same idea in mind, and that plants are not classified arbitrarily? Man has nothing to do with their classification. Nature has attended to all that, giving essential unity with boundless variety, so that the botanist has only to examine plants to learn the harmony of their relations."

This fine lesson charmed me and sent me flying to the woods and meadows in wild enthusiasm. Like everybody else I was always fond of flowers, attracted by their external beauty and purity. Now my eyes were opened to their inner beauty, all alike revealing glorious traces of the thoughts of God, and leading on and on into the infinite cosmos. I wandered away at every opportunity, making long excursions round the lakes, gathering specimens and keeping them fresh in a bucket in my room to study at night after my regular class tasks were learned; for my eyes never closed on the plant glory I had seen.

—John Muir, "The Story of My Boyhood and Youth,"
in *The Wilderness World of John Muir*, ed. Edwin Way Teale
(Boston: Houghton Mifflin Company, 1954), 70

SELECTED RESOURCES FOR CHAPTER EIGHT

Denise Levertov, *The Life Around Us: Selected Poems on Nature* (New York: New Directions Book, 1997).

Jean Mouroux, *The Meaning of Man*, trans. A. H. G. Downes (New York: Image Books, 1961).

Josef Pieper, *Living the Truth* (San Francisco: Ignatius Press, 1989).

·◆·

CHAPTER NINE

THE JOYFUL MYSTERY MADE COMPLETE

"To celebrate a festival means: to live out, for some special occasion and in an uncommon manner, the universal assent to the world as a whole."[1]

"How is it that over 40 years a priest I never before noticed how we are called to be fully engaged, as fellow creatures with the universe and all it contains, in offering praise and thanksgiving to our Creator, through Jesus Christ, His Son, our Lord? To me it seems that our worship, as expressed in both Offertory and Canon, is far ahead of our praxis in ecology and stewardship."[2]

---

[1] Josef Pieper, *In Tune With the World: A Theory of Festivity* (New York: Harcourt, Brace & World, 1965), 23.

[2] Michael Czerny, S.J., "Dimensions of an Integral Ecology," Keynote address at the "Faith, Food, and Environment Symposium" at the University of St. Thomas (November 2014) at https://www.stthomas. edu/media/catholicstudies/center/events/humanandnaturalecology seminar/Czernypaper.pdf.

ANYONE who claims that they are "spiritual, but not religious" is like the one who claims to be hungry but never eats. Eating is the natural activity that satisfies the hungry; religion is the natural activity that satisfies the spiritual. If you are truly immune from any religious practices, then you may have a remarkably imaginative interior life, but you are not spiritual.

It is the most natural of human endeavors to seek the truth about God, and therefore it is only natural to pursue a relationship. As the *Catechism* puts it, "For man is by nature and vocation a religious being . . . and is made to live in communion with God in whom he finds happiness."[3] And while that relationship may take many forms, the common thread weaves back to its origins in recognizing one's status as "being made" by a Maker, a creature with a Creator. As such, "religion denotes properly a relation to God. For it is He to Whom we ought to be bound as to our unfailing principle; to Whom also our choices should be resolutely directed as to our last end; and Whom we lose when we neglect Him by sin, and should recover by believing in Him and confessing our faith."[4] Given the setting we find ourselves in, Thomas says, it only stands to reason that we should do something by way of reverence to God.[5] That something is religion.

And what is that setting? It is an inexhaustible, beautiful cosmos given by a God who supremely loves us. I have already spoken of awe in the presence of the created

[3] CCC 44.
[4] *ST* II-II 81.1.
[5] *ST* II-II 81.1 ad 3.

order and wish to reaffirm, again, its catechetical power in coming to know and love God. Discerning its beauty, its order, its unfolding, its fragility, we can begin to discern with growing confidence a knowledge of God as the one who has made all of this. We read in St. Augustine, "Question the beauty of the earth, question the beauty of the sea, question the beauty of the air distending and diffusing itself, question the beauty of the sky . . . question all these realities. All respond: 'See, we are beautiful.' Their beauty is a profession [*confessio*]. . . . Who made them, if not the Beautiful One who is not subject to change?"[6]

The very passing of things points to the need for something enduring; the fragility of things for something stable. "The world, and man," the Catechism observes, "attest that they contain within themselves neither their first principle nor their final end, but rather that they participate in Being itself, which alone is without origin or end. Thus, in different ways, man can come to know that there exists a reality which is the first cause and final end of all things, a reality 'that everyone calls God'."[7]

While the ecstasy of beauty can bring us to an encounter with the Logos, only revelation can make known fully the God whom we pursue, the God veiled in the beauty of things. The very tentative character of awe, the ambiguity of its disclosure, the weakness of one's comprehension—and the ache, the longing for something all-permanent—all of it prepares the way for a revelation to meet one's deepest aspirations as a person, not merely a creature, of

---

[6] Augustine, *Sermo* 241, 2:PL 38,1134, cited in the CCC 32.
[7] CCC 34.

the cosmos. The heart is dilated by the presence of beauty, and prayer spontaneously fills the void.

Surrounded by a phantasmagoria of splendor, suspended in the sweetest liquor of life, my embodied soul drinks deeply from the waters of being that simultaneously surround it. An inexpressible joy emanates from every facet of my person; together, in sync with a receptivity stretched to the breaking point, a dialectic of praise sounds out from a mutual depth. And still it is not enough. Exhausted by desire, I collapse back into the familiar world of my ordinary experience, remembering, expecting with joyful hope for another epiphany.

Slowly, but surely, with fits and starts, through the rhythm of regret and resolution, this son of Adam, darkened by sin and weakened by habit, claws his way through the things of this world. And again, I ask from the heart of the beauty of things for the grace—and it is given. Seeking the Logos in each valley and vista—it is found. Knocking at the vestibule of every field and forest, my mind is opened: the one I seek seeks me. In the tender compassion of God, the dawn from on high has broken in, and shines on any who wander in darkness and the shadow of death and guides each one of us in an ardent search for peace—as Luke would have it.

The theme runs throughout the Scriptures:

The heavens are telling the glory of God;
and the firmament proclaims his handiwork.
Day to day pours forth speech,
and night to night declares knowledge.
There is no speech, nor are there words;

their voice is not heard;
yet their voice goes out through all the earth,
and their words to the end of the world.
(Ps 19:1–4)

The things of this world have no voice, yet they "speak" of the Logos through whom all things were made. One could follow the wisdom of Job and,

ask the beasts, and they will teach you;
the birds of the air, and they will tell you;
or the plants of the earth, and they will teach you;
and the fish of the sea will declare to you.
Who among all these does not know
that the hand of the Lord has done this?
(Job 12:7–9)

Indeed, "by faith we understand that the world was created by the word of God, so that what is seen was made out of things which do not appear" (Heb 11:3). It was "in him all things were created, in heaven and on earth, visible and invisible, whether thrones or dominions or principalities or authorities—all things were created through him and for him" (Col 1:16). Thus we now see clearly that "ever since the creation of the world his invisible nature, namely, his eternal power and deity, has been clearly perceived in the things that have been made" (Rom 1:20). And thus together, in a spirit of sacrifice and in union with all of creation, we affirm that, "Thou art the Lord, thou alone; thou hast made heaven, the heaven of heavens, with all their host, the earth and all that is on it, the seas and all that is in them; and thou preservest all of them; and the host of heaven worships thee" (Neh 9:6). We do this through public worship so that all "see what is the plan of the mystery hidden for ages in God who created all things" (Eph 3:9).

Knowing that, "Thou art the Lord, thou alone; thou hast made heaven, the heaven of heavens, with all their host, the earth and all that is on it, the seas and all that is in them; and thou preservest all of them; and the host of heaven worships thee" (Acts 17:25). And that it is, "in him we live and move and have our being," we celebrate and proclaim the fact that, "he chose us in him before the foundation of the world, that we should be holy and blameless before him; he destine us in love to be his sons through Jesus Christ, according to the purpose of his will" (Acts 17:28; Eph 1:4–5). Indeed, this was His "plan for the fullness of time, to unite all things in Him, things in heaven and things on earth" (Eph 1:5–6, 10). At the Eucharistic table we gather as adopted children of the Father, in the Son, who "is the image of the invisible God, the first-born of all creation" (Col 1:15).

Simply by Baptism, then, we are united to creation in a manner like no other creature, for united to the Logos in a spirit of divine adoption, we are now one with Him and are now alive in Him, and thus we are enabled "by the mercies of God, to present [our] bodies as a living sacrifice, holy and acceptable to God, which is [our] spiritual worship" (Rom 12:1). Whether we are to become in our embodied selves a "living sacrifice" as St. Paul says or "living stones" as St. Peter (the living stone) calls it, whatever the metaphor, the consensus is clear that in our very bodies we are making complete His plan of creation, for "we are His workmanship, created in Christ Jesus for good works" (Eph 2:10). And thus it is that, "he is not far from each one of us, for 'In him we live and move and have our being'; as even some of [the] poets have said, 'For we are indeed his offspring'" (Acts 17:27–28).

It is as beholders of the Logos and bearers of the Son that we have the warrant to pray, precisely in a spontaneous exercise of religion:

> It is truly right to give you thanks, truly just to give you glory, Father, most holy, for you are the one God living and true, existing before all ages and abiding for all eternity, dwelling in unapproachable light; yet you, who alone are good, the source of life, have made all that is, so that you might fill your creatures with blessings and bring joy to many of them by the glory of your light. And so, in your presence are countless hosts of Angels, who serve you day and night and, gazing upon the glory of your face, glorify you without ceasing. With them we, too, confess your name in exultation, giving voice to every creature under heaven as we acclaim. . . .[8]

Integral ecology is doxology; there is no simpler way to put it. In loving the things of creation out of love for the Creator, we express in the smallest of ways the divine

---

[8] Roman Missal, Eucharistic Prayer IV.

privilege as a steward of His earth, the divine privilege as adopted daughters and sons of the Owner. And so that "we might live no longer for ourselves but for Him who died and rose again for us, He sent the Holy Spirit from you, Father, as the first fruits for those who believe, so that, bringing to perfection His work in the world, He might sanctify creation to the full."[9]

Christ dawns on me and in the daybreak of faith I warm to the vision that I have glimpsed in a facet of the universe what will only be fulfilled in the face of God. By the sheer grace of faith I come to see that the Logos has taken my flesh and by gently leading me by the hand away from all that is familiar gives me my sight that I may see "all things clearly," beholding the face of God who now beholds me.

It is not through some kind of Manichean renunciation of our earthly status that we rise to give praise to the Maker of the earth and the Redeemer of heaven. We do not adopt some ghostly standing or seek to create a paranormal space in which we may meet the Lord. The primary movement of the Eucharist is that of divine descent. The hidden God comes and offers Himself, again, in the form of bread and wine, to be in communion with His friends of the earth. He knows His children all too well, knows that when we are hungry the mere "idea" of a meal will not do. Once again, Christianity is not a philosophy, a set of ideas or attitudes maintained in the labyrinthine ways of one's mind. And so it is not the idea of God that satisfies the deepest longing, but God Himself. He de-

---

[9] Ibid.

scends to us in one of the most powerful means of union: He comes as food; He comes as drink.

Eucharist is the fulfillment of the practice of integral ecology. Carried by the medium of bread and wine, made Christ by the power of the Spirit, all of lower creation is brought to its completion in Him. The doxology is lifted from the ranks of the creatures themselves.

The primary movement is that of descent, "like the dew fall," but the secondary movement, so close in significance, is an ascent, indeed a communion of my embodied soul now raised in union with the living body of His Church. The triple wound begins to be healed, as the medicine of immortality wends its way through my broken being.

Between myself and God a reconciliation begins: a recovered coin is happily announced; a wayward sheep is carried back into the fold; a son returns to the arms of his father and a daughter is restored in her dignity. The intellect is made lighter by faith, warmed with the intelligence of a Divine acknowledgement that begins to fill the fissures of one's prior understanding with the precious balm of grace. In now knowing the Logos of creation as my Lord, Redeemer, and friend, I see that the green pastures to which He once led me are the places He now seeks to greet me; the vistas, His call to renewal. I know His counsel under the stars and His care in the verdant valleys of spring. Nature is no longer merely an aesthetic moment but an intimate one. The echoes of an interior monologue merge into a spiritual dialogue, and a wildlife sanctuary becomes what it was always meant to be: the sacred space of divine encounter. "Therefore, behold, I will allure

[you], and bring [you] into the wilderness, and speak tenderly to [you]" (Hos 2:14). Swept along in a spontaneous reverie of prayer and praise, I am freed from the burden of preoccupation. Stepping forward into the fuller world of religion, I am now impelled to bring with me all the gifts of the universe "Abba" has given to me, and return them in gratitude at the dining table of communion.

My will, too, is made more supple. Once stiff with self-assertion, I allow myself to be moved by another, moved by the Other, and slowly the flex of love makes my movements more graceful, my steps more beautiful. Little by little, I begin to speak for myself, to speak from the self now loved deeply in Christ, and the unruly forces of impulse begin to be seen for what they are—not the expression of any animal need, but the insistent urgency of fretful demands. In allowing myself to become the full stature of a man in Christ, I, at the same time, become a child in Him.

Between myself and others, an alienation dissipates as the morning star rises in my heart (2 Pet 1:19). The circle of concern extends now to the edges of humanity itself, for the Logos discerned in the Heavens is the Redeemer of man, not just Christians. It is as ridiculous to hoard the beauty of nature as it is to restrict the encounter with His love. A banquet is given and strangers are made friends, late-comers receive a full wage, baskets overflow to their brims. I am no longer indifferent to the circumstances of my neighbor because my neighbor is now a companion keeper of His earth, a potential heir of the Owner. Justice probes to the root of the problem, for it, too, like faith, is not a mere idea or sentiment. I can no longer profess a love for my neighbors while ignoring the conditions in which they seek to flourish. For all of us are yoked to the one earth we share now, and, in light of the one Redeemer we seek, are united in a common cause in both origin and end. And so I no longer resent the presence of the poor, nor see in them a mere indictment of my lifestyle. But as the message goes out to all the earth, it now speaks through the faces of the peoples who inhabit it. I cannot love the Logos of creation and ignore the human family with whom He chooses to dwell, for whom He chooses to die. Nor can I pretend that my concern at a distance, in thought and word alone, can dismiss me from my obligations to care for the earth we now share. The one earth speaks of His one love for the one people we are called to serve.

And finally, in Him, the blessed world of things is once again an occasion of sheer delight. The banquet of graces He lays out before me every morning and night is a foretaste of what is to come. The only world I now wish to renounce is the one of my own disordered making. In Christ, the earth becomes a tabernacle and the creatures, indeed the very stones, ministers in His temple. The protagonist of Myles Connolly's fictional classic speaks well of the matter:

> Without Christ we would be little more than bacteria breeding on a pebble in space, or glints of ideas in a whirling void of abstractions. Because of Him, I can stand here out under this cold immensity and know that my infinitesimal pulse-beats and acts and thoughts are of more importance than this whole show of a universe. Only for Him,

I would be crushed beneath the weight of all these worlds. Only for Him, I would tumble dazed into the gaping chasms of space and time. Only for Him, I would be confounded before the awful fertility and intricacy of all life. Only for Him, I would be the merest of animalcules crawling on the merest of motes in a frigid Infinity. . . . Blah!— for the immensity of space! Blah!—for those who would have me a microcosm in the meaningless tangle of an endless evolution! I'm no microcosm. I, too, am a Son of God![10]

The language still captivates me and eloquently expresses the conversion of a Green Thomist on the precipice of being. Integral ecology completes the circle of glory, for in serving Christ in His universe, the universe is brought to Christ. The glorious stuff of the world is made holy in offering it to Him from whom all things came in the very beginning. In Him, my dominion over creation is made perfect, for I adopt the original dominion of the Creator of all things: I behold it all in contemplative splendor and announce it as good, indeed, very good.

Not just in contemplative moments, but in the practical life, too, the circle of salvation is made more complete, for the use of creation is now ordered to His glory, not gain. In temperance, we modify our consumption of things, even renouncing some altogether, to live a modesty that reflects a divine friendship. In fortitude, we maintain a horizon of hope against the seemingly insurmountable odds opposing

[10] Myles Connolly, *Mr. Blue* (New York: Cluny Media, 2015), 35.

us. Prudence seeks a more modest aim while at the same time extends its horizon of concern. Justice now includes everything that is due the maker and sustainer of all things. To will the good of the other, then, extends to the creatures themselves. And all of my movements become a symphony of praise in the anthem of creation and redemption: frost and chill, ice and snow, dew and rain, all creatures praise and exalt Him above all forever!

*　*　*　*　*

The Eucharist brings to fruition the accomplishment of integrated, graced living and points to the eschatological fulfillment of the arrangement of the world. Some may wonder if there will be animals in the heavenly dwelling promised by the Father. For myself, there is no doubt that there will be animals in heaven: we call them saints. "For that which rises must be an animal if it is to be a man."[11] Redeemed in Christ and now renewed in their glorified bodies, the saints will be those blessed citizens of incorruptible communion who enjoy in their ensouled, glorified flesh what they were called out to be since the creation of the world. For the separated human soul, being created as the form of the human body, "is not wholly at rest, as regards the desirer, since it does not possess that good in every way that it would wish to possess it [namely, as united to a body]."[12] Wherefore, it is fitting for the complete beatitude of the human being, that the soul be united to its body. Such souls "will be lightsome, incapa-

---

[11] *SCG* IV 84, 14.
[12] *ST* I-II 4.5 ad 5.

ble of suffering, without difficulty and labor in movement, and most perfectly perfected by its form."[13]

As for the other creatures? Thomas himself expresses little doubt on the matter: animals and plants will pass away in the new order which lies on the other side of the general resurrection. Thomas argues that the motion of the celestial bodies will cease; and the lower orders of creatures, which he believed to be dependent upon the movement of such bodies, will also pass away. He also suggests that the purpose of creatures will have been served. Being created exclusively for the use of human beings (who would then be perfected in beatitude), other creatures will be effectively dismissed as irrelevant in the new order of blessedness.[14]

Not surprisingly, his reflections on the eschatological conditions of creation and the human person are enmeshed in the contemporary theories of celestial causality of his day. And for this reason Thomas' comments regarding the lower orders of creation and the embodied human being in the eschaton seem insufficiently developed and are often less than satisfying.[15] This leaves Thomists with important decisions to make. One could pass over in silence his remarks on the nature of things in the eschaton, strategically protecting his thought from criticisms effectively raised in contemporary circles. This would treat the living tradition of Thomistic thought as a museum piece of mere historical curiosity, or worse, as a warehouse of decorative

---

[13] *SCG* IV 86, 6.
[14] See *SCG* IV 97.5; *Compendium*, 170; *Supplementum* 91.5.
[15] See, for example, *Supplementum* 81.4; *De potentia* 5.9.

trappings for lingering ideologies. The second way would be to shackle the Thomistic tradition to outdated empirical observations in order to disqualify Thomism as a legitimate contributor, thus severing ourselves from perennial wisdom. The third route is that of Green Thomists, who are willing to imagine a return to the perennial wisdom of St. Thomas and to dialogue with contemporary insights in order to refine and further correct defects that have accrued along the way. The path ahead seems clear.

Such a path will not be a matter of redeeming lower creation, for the lower orders of creation were not affected by sin and thus they are non-contestants in the drama of redemption. Thomas, following Augustine, seems reluctant to extend the notion that "*apokaradokia*," the eager expectation, of *Romans* 8:19 describes the animal and plant kingdoms of the earth.[16] Green Thomists are reluctant to speak of any redemption for lower creation, for to do so would be to suggest that the created order is now somehow inescapably mired in darkness and error. Such a direction would cut us off from the light of created natures, the first tutors in the faith, and sever Thomism and the culture to which it aspires from its rootedness in the earth. "This was the error of the Manichees," Augustine says, and Green Thomists are not about to repeat the mistake.[17]

---

[16] Thomas Aquinas, *Lecture 4* in *Commentary on the Letter of Saint Paul to the Romans*, trans. Fr. Fabian Larcher, O.P. (Lander, WY: The Aquinas Institute, 2012), 323–331. Contrast with Joseph A. Fitzmyer, S.J., *The Anchor Bible: Romans* (New York: Doubleday, 1993), 504–511.

[17] Augustine, *Propositions from the Epistle to the Romans*, 53, in Paula Fredriksen Landes, *Augustine on Romans: Propositions from the Epistle to the Romans; Unfinished Commentary on the Epistle to the Romans* (Chico, CA: Scholars Press, 1982), 23.

Declining to extend the redemptive narrative to include those creatures for whom redemption is not relevant is not to jettison such creatures into ontic oblivion. In fact, it provides an opportunity to retrieve them in newer ways. Creatures could have standing in the eschaton not out of some soteriological reason, but because God's eternal goodness and generosity calls for it. And it is precisely Thomas' genius in outlining the manner in which we have come through creation to encounter this utterly generous God who opens a way for a restoration of creatures in beatitude.

It would seem only fitting, to borrow a method of argument especially dear to St. Thomas, to take his indefatigable defense of things and their capacity to disclose the reality of God and use it as a basis for further reflection. If "heaven" were understood as the fullest expression of divine glory, every smattering of creation and its kinds could be somehow sustained in a manner beyond all comprehending, not for the sake of a humanity who has any use for such things, but for the sake of a humanity who can love such things—because they completely love the One from whom all good things come. We can differ about the details, yet be confident with St. Thomas that the lasting and final kingdom could be so best arranged as to redound to the glory of the Father and His adopted family. Once given the privileged task to till and to keep His earth, we would enjoy the fully infused, supernatural task of participated dominion and through Him, with Him, and in Him, simply love Him.

Green Thomists are willing to imagine that by beholding creation refracted in a *plenum gloriae* of the Creator, one could contemplate more completely the One beholding us. God's goodness of its very nature seeks to communicate itself, and He loves every existing creature with a love that bestows upon them a goodness which could in heaven be more richly understood.[18] If Thomas says that each creature, as God's work of art,[19] bears now in its liveliness (however dim and dark)[20] the vestige of the Father in its substance, the Son in its species, and the Spirit in its communion;[21] that "the whole world is nothing other than a vast representation of the divine Wisdom in the mind of the Father;"[22] that God is now in all things entirely and in each of them, just as the soul is entirely in each part of the body,[23] and is so in His essence, power, and presence in a most intimate way;[24] if the very diversity of being is more perfectly suited to manifest His Divine glory;[25] and that to "subtract something from the perfection of creatures is to remove something from the perfection of the divine virtue;"[26] if he argues that God's power is "more conspicuously shown" in His preserving all things as opposed to annihilating them;[27] and if he allows that the divine motivation for the Incarnation may include the

---

[18] *ST* I 20.2.
[19] *ST* I 91.3.
[20] *SCG* III 26, n3633, cited in Torrell, 65.
[21] *ST* I 45.7.
[22] *In Iohannem* I, 10, lect. 5, n. 136, cited in Torrell, 66.
[23] *ST* I 8.2 ad 3.
[24] *ST* I 8.1 and 3.
[25] *ST* I 47.1
[26] *SCG* III 69, 2445-46.
[27] *ST* I 104.4 ad 1.

coronation (consummation) of the whole universe;[28] and, finally, if he proposes that having a glorious body is necessary for our well-being in complete beatitude;[29] we can fruitfully wonder in faithful joy what the divine recreation may come to mean when He makes all things new in the beatitude of a new heaven and earth.

"At the end," Pope Francis says, "we will find ourselves face to face with the infinite beauty of God":

> and be able to read with admiration and happiness the mystery of the universe, which with us will share in unending plenitude. Even now we are journeying towards the sabbath of eternity, the new Jerusalem, towards our common home in heaven. Jesus says: "I make all things new" (Rev 21:5). Eternal life will be a shared experience of awe, in which each creature, resplendently transfigured, will take its rightful place and have something to give those poor men and women who will have been liberated once and for all.[30]

Every people, every age, tries to get right with God, tries to come to respond to the author who is discerned in the text of the universe. Christians, Catholics in particular, are no exception to the universal desire for adoration. We get right with God by doing what we believe He asked us to do: we offer the Holy Sacrifice of the Mass.

---

[28] *In Sent.* d.1.q.1 a.3, cited in Torrell, 72. Also, *ST* III 6.1.
[29] *ST* I-II 4.5 and 6.
[30] *LS*, no. 243.

Gratitude is the permanent posture one takes before the joyful mystery of creation. It swells from the deepest recesses of awe and overflows into an abundance of various qualities of lightsomeness: there is the intense feeling of *euphoria*—a kind of passive participation of being held by beauty. There is the earnest effort to behold beauty and the desire to live in sync with its flourishing, namely, *eudaimonia*. There is then the impulse that gives way to *latria*, the effort to utter one's own words before the Word. And finally, by the sheer surprise of grace, *eucharistia*, by which the Word becomes one's own word of thanksgiving and praise. Whether this unfolds in a moment of insight or a lifetime of labor, the glorious transit of creation is made complete: through grace, with grace, in grace.

How is it indeed that after forty years as a priest a man comes to see the connections between creation and Christ, the soil and the Spirit? Perhaps it is by that Spirit who "over the bent world broods, with warm breast, and ah! bright wings!" Perhaps it is through that One who teaches us what is truly, in all truth, a Kingfisher.

SELECTED READINGS FOR CHAPTER NINE

On Atheism as the Exception

Of all the illusions of the world of artifacts and constructs, the most facile and the most palpably false is the claim that the awareness of God's presence—in our inept phrase, "believing in God"—is the peculiarity of certain individuals, an opinion contingently held by some members of the species. The obverse it true. It is the blindness to God's presence that is exceptional. Humans, as a species, through the millennia and all over the globe, have been worshippers of the Holy. The awareness of God's presence is and ever has been the most persistent specific trait of our species being. Even the secular anthropologists use the evidence of worship as the distinguishing mark of a human rather than simply higher primate presence. Both empirically and eidetically, humans are beings who know God. The real question is not the very recent one, why some humans believe, but rather why some humans profess to be blind to God's presence. . . . As for accounting for the fact of worship itself, the explanation most readily available and most parsimonious is far simpler: humans worship because the evident presence of God in nature and history is the most primordial given of lived experience.

—Erazim Kohák, *The Embers and the Stars:*
A Philosophical Inquiry into the Moral Sense of Nature
(Chicago: The University of Chicago Press, 1984), 185–186

On the Meaning of the Universe in the Eucharist

The Sacraments are a privileged way in which nature is taken up by God to become a means of mediating supernatural life. Through our worship of God, we are invited to embrace the world on a different plane. Water, oil, fire and colors are taken up in all their symbolic power and incorporated in our act of praise. The hand that blesses is an instrument of God's love and a reflection of the closeness of Jesus Christ, who came to accompany us on the journey of life. Water poured over the body of a child in Baptism is a sign of new life. Encountering God does not mean fleeing from this world or turning our back on nature. This is especially clear in the spirituality of the Christian East. "Beauty, which in the East is one of the best loved names expressing the divine harmony and the model of humanity transfigured, appears everywhere: in the shape of a church, in the sounds, in the colors, in the lights, in the scents." For Christians, all the creatures of the material universe find their true meaning in the incarnate Word, for the Son of God has incorporated in his person part of the material world, planting in it a seed of definitive transformation. "Christianity does not reject matter. Rather, bodiliness is considered in all its value in the liturgical act, whereby the human body is disclosed in its inner nature as a temple of the Holy Spirit and is united with the Lord Jesus, who Himself took a body for the world's salvation."

It is in the Eucharist that all that has been created finds its greatest exaltation. Grace, which tends to manifest itself tangibly, found unsurpassable expression when God Himself became man and gave Himself as food for His creatures. The Lord, in the culmination of the mystery of the Incarnation, chose to reach our intimate depths through a fragment of matter. He comes not from above, but from within, He comes that we might find Him in this world of ours. In the Eucharist, fullness is already achieved; it is the living center of the universe, the overflowing core of love and of inexhaustible life. Joined to the incarnate Son, present in the Eucharist, the whole cosmos gives thanks to God. Indeed the Eucharist is itself an act of cosmic love: "Yes, cosmic! Because even when it is celebrated on the humble altar of a country church, the Eucharist is always in some way celebrated on the altar of the world." The Eucharist joins heaven and earth; it embraces and penetrates all creation. The world which came forth from God's hands returns to Him in blessed and undivided adoration: in the bread of the Eucharist, "creation is projected towards divinization, towards the holy wedding feast, towards unification with the Creator Himself." Thus, the Eucharist is also a source of light and motivation for our concerns for the environment, directing us to be stewards of all creation.

On Sunday, our participation in the Eucharist has special importance. Sunday, like the Jewish Sabbath, is meant to be a day which heals our relationships with God, with ourselves, with others and with the world. Sunday is the day of the Resurrection, the "first day" of the new creation, whose first fruits are the Lord's risen humanity, the pledge of the final transfiguration of all created reality. It also proclaims "man's eternal rest in God." In this way, Christian spirituality incorporates the value of relaxation and festivity. We tend to demean contemplative rest as something unproductive and unnecessary, but this is to do away with the very thing which is most important about work: its meaning. We are called to include in our work a dimension of receptivity and gratuity, which is quite different from mere inactivity. Rather, it is another way of working, which forms part of our very essence. It protects human action from becoming empty activism; it also prevents that unfettered greed and sense of isolation which make us seek personal gain to the detriment of all else. The law of weekly rest forbade work on the seventh day, "so that your ox and your donkey may have rest, and the son of your maidservant, and the stranger, may be refreshed" (Ex 23:12). Rest opens our eyes to the larger picture and gives us renewed sensitivity to the rights of others. And so the day of rest, centered on the Eucharist, sheds its light on the whole week, and motivates us to greater concern for nature and the poor.

—Pope Francis, *LS*, nos. 235–237

On the Resurrection of the Individual's Body

Since the soul is united to the body as its form, and since each form has the right matter corresponding to it, the body to which the soul will be reunited must be of the same nature and species as was the body laid down by the soul at death. At the resurrection the soul will not resume a celestial or ethereal body, or the body of some animal as certain people fancifully prattle. No, it will resume a human body made up of flesh and bones, and equipped with the same organs it now possesses.

—St. Thomas Aquinas, *Light of Faith [The Compendium of Theology]* (Manchester, NH: Sophia Institute Press, 2003), 153

On Hope in the Heavenly Feast

In the meantime, we come together to take charge of this home which has been entrusted to us, knowing that all the good which exists here will be taken up into the heavenly feast. In union with all creatures, we journey through this land seeking God, for "if the world has a beginning and if it has been created, we must enquire who gave it this beginning, and who was its Creator." Let us sing as we go. May our struggles and our concern for this planet never take away the joy of our hope.

—Pope Francis, *LS*, no. 244

SELECTED RESOURCES FOR CHAPTER NINE

On Earth as it is in Heaven: Cultivating a Contemporary Theology of Creation, ed. David V. Meconi, S.J., (Grand Rapids, MI: Eerdmans, 2016).

Erazim Kohák, *The Embers and the Stars: A Philosophical Inquiry into the Moral Sense of Nature* (Chicago: The University of Chicago Press, 1984).

CPSIA information can be obtained
at www.ICGtesting.com
Printed in the USA
BVHW030247300822
645808BV00005B/7/J

9 781945 125614